A CRASH COURSE
IN FINANCE

A **SOHO** Crash Course Book

small office home office

A CRASH COURSE IN FINANCE

Understand and control your finances, maximize your profits, and create true wealth in your business

DAVID H. "ANDY" BANGS
& ANDI AXMAN

Adams Media Corporation
Holbrook, Massachusetts

Published by
Adams Media Corporation
260 Center Street, Holbrook, MA 02343. U. S. A.

ISBN: 1-58062-483-9

Printed in Canada.

J I H G F E D C B A

Library of Congress Cataloging-in-Publication Data
Bangs, David H.
A crash course in financing / by David H. Bangs and Andi Axman.
p.   cm.
ISBN 1-58062-483-9
1. Small business--Finance. I. Axman, Andi. II. Title
HG4027.7 .B345   2001
658.15′92--dc21   00-0954004

This publication is designed to provide accurate and authoritative information with
regard to the subject matter covered. It is sold with the understanding that the pub-
lisher is not engaged in rendering legal, accounting, or other professional advice. If
legal advice or other expert assistance is required, the services of a competent professional person should be sought.
— From a *Declaration of Principles* jointly adopted by a Committee of the
American Bar Association and a Committee of Publishers and Associations

Cover illustration © Artville

This book is available at quantity discounts for bulk purchases.
For information, call 1-800-872-5627.

Visit our exciting Web site at *www.businesstown.com*

Acknowledgments

We'd like to give special thanks to the following:

- Our spouses, Lacey Bangs and Mark Goldstein, for their loving support and help.
- Our Wonderdogs—Thud, a black Labrador retriever, and Ruby, a Chesapeake Bay retriever—for their wagging tails and constant companionship.
- Jere Calmes, our editor at Adams Media Corporation, for encouraging us to write this book.
- All of our clients and colleagues, for sharing their experiences with us—without which we could not have written this book.

Table of Contents

Section II: *Getting Money for Your Business*

Section III: *Making the Most of Your Money*

Section IV: *Growing Your Business*

Introduction

Although we call this book *A Crash Course in Finance,* it is not a textbook. Far from it—there are plenty of excellent textbooks in print that go into great detail about the concepts that underlie financing. We are more concerned with providing practical advice on how to handle the financing issues business owners face. Everyone is affected by financing in one way or another, whether as owner, employee, customer, or vendor. Financing makes a big difference for every business. Make the proper financing decisions and your business will grow. Make the wrong decisions and your business could fail.

There is nothing mysterious about financing. Financing is concerned with the acquisition and use of resources. A start-up needs to raise capital, cash, and credit to get on its feet. A going business finances equipment in part by borrowing from the vendor or a bank. A growing business begins to run out of cash and decides to finance the growth by seeking new capital and a bigger line of credit. Financing techniques range from boot-strapping to the most complicated public stock or bond offerings. This book concentrates on the most appropriate financing techniques for small businesses.

Learning finance involves learning a new language. You already manage cash flow, understand budgeting (including capital budgeting), and are familiar with financial statements. Cash-flow management involves matching the inflow and outflow of cash based on rational assumptions. Think of the ways college students balance their cash flow: inflow is derived from parents and grandparents, part-time jobs, selling used textbooks, borrowing from pals. Outflows are matched to these sources—a concert, a ski trip, tuition, new books. This is cash-flow management at its purest.

Your budget controls expenditures. In business this is a more formal process than making sure you deposit your paycheck and keep your bills up to date. The concept is identical: don't spend more than you earn, and (if possible) set some cash aside for a rainy day. Capital budgeting is exemplified by saving for a major purchase, setting priorities on how to spend your money in order to reach long-term goals.

You will become familiar with technical terms such as leverage, debt load, risk, and exit strategy. The terminology of finance has to be precise since it is so central to the conduct of organizations. Knowing the lingo will help you communicate with your bankers, who will provide a major piece of your financing puzzle.

We assume that you are currently practicing a few basic financial techniques:

- *You have a clear bookkeeping system* to gather the information you need to make good financial decisions. We don't intend to show you how to keep your books.
- *You use accurate, timely financial statements* to manage your business. While we will refer to your balance sheet, profit-and-loss (or income) statement, and cash-flow statements and budgets, this book cannot teach you how to read them. There are plenty of good courses available to you through Small Business Development Centers, local colleges, and even brokerage houses.
- *Your accountant or other financial advisor* has set up your accounting so that it helps you figure out capital needs (including timing), operating cash needs, and growth capital needs. This means using historical and current financial statements and pro forma or projected financial statements to bolster and enhance your decision-making powers.

In Appendix Three, we include information on some of the less complicated, but extremely helpful, financial ratios. The math involved in using them is exceedingly simple (the numbers you plug in can be found right on your financial statements), and we encourage you to put these ratios to work. We are strong believers in ratio analysis, perhaps due to Andy's banking and entrepreneurial experience.

Informal measures of financial health abound. Some common negatives are posting losses, running out of cash, trouble meeting payroll, grumbling vendors, and postponing—again and again—investment in plant and equipment. Positive indicators include taking discounts, making consistent profits, and having investment bankers drop by just to chat. Equivocal measures needing scrutiny include chronic large cash balances, rapidly growing sales, and uneven cash flows.

Finally, we will run through a lengthy list of financing sources. Some are conventional: your own resources, banks, outside investors. Some are somewhat unconventional: credit circles, customer financing, and recondite government agencies with programs targeted to particular needs. As a wise manager you will want to be aware of the range, requirements, and accessibility of many financing sources.

A note on our credentials: Andy has been a banker, a successful entrepreneur, and best-selling author of 15 books. This book is the fourth he's cowritten with Andi, who has extensive experience as a freelance writer specializing in business topics. She owned her own small publishing business and was once involved in restoring an old mill. Both Andy and Andi do a great deal of volunteer work and sit on a number of nonprofit and business boards.

SECTION I:

Laying the Groundwork to Finance Your Business

1

How Do You Prepare for Start-up?

Investors (you, bankers, or anyone else who lends money) want to be sure that their investment makes good financial sense—that is, the risks and rewards are acceptable, the investment will help the business grow, and the investment will pay off in a reasonable length of time. This is tough enough for any business, but especially tough for a start-up. (Turnarounds are much like start-ups so if you are seeking financing to turn a failing business around, you will face the same problems.)

The greatest single problem is finding information to support your financing proposal. This is an area where the Internet (Net) is invaluable. Throughout this book we will refer to Web sites that help you gain the results you seek. If you are not on the Net, you are making a major mistake; although you can still access the information you need, the work will be harder than it has to be.

Start-ups need business plans. They need them even more than going businesses do, since there is no track record for the investor to rely on. Your business plan helps you to model your business concept, test ideas, predict costs, play "what if," and examine different scenarios and assumptions. More than that, it helps the investor understand what you have in mind and why your business will be successful. While a financial model (your projected balance sheet, income statements, and cash-flow budgets) is only a model, it is a lot better than unsubstantiated hope. Don't forget,

3

you are the biggest investor in your start-up: your time, energy, assets, and dreams are on the line. The financial statements will help you make better business decisions.

By failing to prepare you are preparing to fail.
BENJAMIN FRANKLIN

In order to come up with a good business plan you need information about how your business will operate. Unfortunately, it's difficult to get good operating data for a start-up. The standard sources of such data are based on averaging operating data for businesses that have already survived the start-up phase. Those businesses are of all sizes, ages, and locations. What does a start-up restaurant in Portsmouth, New Hampshire, have in common with an established restaurant in Houston or Los Angeles or Chicago? Not much beyond being in the same industry. However, there is a source on the Internet that will get you started. Visit *www.morebusiness.com/tools/bizstats* to compare your business's projected figures to trade or industry—but keep in mind that the base is not formulated using start-up numbers.

Once you have your projected revenues and expenses, check with your accountant to see how well they fit what your banker's or another sophisticated investor's ideas of what your financial picture should be. Or better yet, sit down with your banker, show him or her your early numbers, and solicit his or her advice on how to make your projections as realistic as

Some of the most successful technology companies were started by university students. Bill Gates dropped out of Harvard University to join Paul Allen to pursue their software programming efforts full-time. The result was Microsoft. And Yahoo's Jerry Yang and David Filo were Stanford University graduate students when they decided to turn their Web site directory into a company. It's no wonder that venture capitalists have helped colleges create competitions for the best business plan; about 30 universities have such face-offs. MIT's competition produced Akamai Technologies, the Cambridge, Massachusetts, firm that boasts a market valuation of $25 billion. (*Fortune*, "Battle of the Business Plan," January 24, 2000)

possible. This shows that you are serious about your business and helps build credibility with your banker.

There are more than 35,000 trade associations in the United States. Join the one that most closely mirrors yours. You can also visit comparable businesses and ask the owners about their start-up experience. The Net is a great source for this kind of information. For example, Business Town's Web site (*www.businesstown.com*) has a dandy list of trade associations that you can query. Suppose you plan to start a retail business. Follow the link to the National Retail Federation (*www.nrf.com*) and you'll find a wealth of information, including links to your state's retail trade association. If you can't leverage that into good data for your start-up you shouldn't be in business at all!

Start with your proposed costs. It is easier to pin down start-up expenses than to estimate start-up revenues and cash flow—and the expense side gives you a clue to the level of revenues you will need to make your venture work. The Small Business Administration (*www.sbaonline.sba.gov*) has a useful form for calculating your start-up expenses, including those one-time costs and some operating expenses that can be calculated in advance. (See Appendix One.) And while you are figuring out your start-up expenses, keep track of how you arrive at each figure. A quote from a supplier will be more useful than a guess, and will help you win the battle for credibility with your investors.

Scott Balmer, 74, the founder and chairman of Power Save International in Tamarac, Florida, expected it would take three years to develop and market the technology for his energy-saving co-generators. In fact, it took 10. At one point, he went so far into debt that the lender foreclosed on his house, and he and his wife had to move to an apartment. They spent all their savings, cashed in all their insurance policies, and were broke. Balmer has since gotten back on his feet, in part by bringing in other investors. He has also appointed a younger CEO, to assuage any investors' fears about continuity. (*Business Week*, "Senior Start-ups," August 14, 2000)

Plan ahead: It wasn't raining when Noah built the ark.
RICHARD CUSHING

The Women's Technology Cluster is a nonprofit incubator in San Francisco that's home to 10 new Internet and technology companies where women hold a major equity stake. Launched in February 1999, the Cluster is a kind of learning laboratory for start-ups. Start-up founders get mentoring and support from experienced business leaders. Entrepreneurs share office resources as well as information, contacts, and support. At the core of the Cluster is the idea that you're more likely to be successful if you don't go it alone. (*Fast Company*, "Learning and Change," December 1999)

The learning curve for start-ups is very steep. Even if you have a lot of experience in the business there will be unexpected challenges. In our experience no start-up ever goes as planned. Your best defense—and this will affect your financing plans—is to talk with as many other business owners who have gone through start-ups similar to yours as you can find. Ask your banker, accountant, friends, trade associations, and other informed folks. While much of the advice you receive will be anecdotal and perhaps not pertinent to your situation, much will be relevant. More important, it will make you aware of the kinds of challenges that you may have to address. The key question to ask is: If you knew then what you know now, what would you have done differently? While every start-up is different, there is a common set of problems they all face.

It is one of the most beautiful compensations of this life that no man can sincerely try to help another without helping himself.
RALPH WALDO EMERSON

Start-ups face lots of competition. You have to know who these competitors are in order to satisfy this important question: Is there enough room in this market for another player? You can get data from trade associations on how large a market is needed to support your hardware store. If there are two stores in your area already, will there be room for you? What if one of them is a "big-box" store, like Home Depot or Wal-Mart? By paying attention to what the competition does you may be able to find an underserved niche that can become a profitable market for you. It always comes down to marketing! How can you attract and satisfy the customers you compete for? Are there enough of them? This is vitally important in making your sales projections.

The first questions investors ask are "How much?" and "What for?" Therefore, you must push a detailed cash-flow projection (a cash budget) to determine how much cash your business needs. Go out, month by month, until the cash flow turns positive. The deepest point of cumulative negative cash flow gives you a clue about the size of investment needed to make your business work. The rule of thumb is then to double that figure, thus ensuring that surprises and shortfalls will be covered. If you are wise you'll also prepare a personal cash flow to determine what your own financial needs will be and make the decisions about where that cash will come from before draining funds from your new venture.

They know enough who know how to learn.

HENRY ADAMS

Write your own business plan. Get help if you need it. Small Business Development Centers (SBDCs) were created to help you with business planning and financing (among their other purposes—see page 86, Chapter 7, for more information on SBDCs). Go to *www.smallbiz.suny.edu* for a listing of SBDCs on the Net. Then get outsiders to critique the plan before presenting it to outside investors.

As a sideline to her own $6 million business, Capitol Concierge, which is based in Washington, D.C., Marge Naylor offers a one-day seminar to aspiring corporate concierges. In the first two years that she offered the course, 15 would-be concierges traveled from as far away as Brazil and shelled out up to $3,000 to attend. Naylor's instruction covers topics like how to budget expenses and recruit and retain customers. More than half of Naylor's students have gone on to start concierge companies or incorporate them into existing businesses. (*Inc.*, "Concierge Makes Hay in Corporate Fields," September 1, 1998)

Back in 1982, when he and three others started Sun Microsystems Inc., Scott McNealy, then 27, borrowed $15,000 in start-up capital from his father. Originally in charge of manufacturing for the budding business, McNealy didn't know a thing about high-tech. Today McNealy is recognized as a visionary in the high-tech industry and Sun Microsystems has earned a reputation as a leading provider of heavy-duty, technologically sophisticated computers known as workstations and servers that use the Unix operating system, generally considered more reliable than Microsoft's operating system. Sun is also the market leader in setting up systems for Internet companies. (*Entrepreneur,* August 2000, page 85)

Be aware that almost nobody wants to finance start-ups. Good start-up financing sources begin with your own assets and those of family and friends. If your idea is good, then you should have no qualms about giving your family and friends a chance to invest in your business. If you are queasy about asking, it's a tip that perhaps your idea isn't that good.

Life is not easy for any of us. But what of that? We must have perseverance and, above all, confidence in ourselves. We must believe that we are gifted for something, and this thing, at whatever cost, must be attained.
MARIE CURIE

If yours is a B2B business, few going concerns will want to do business with you. Reliability and reputation are extremely important in business-to-business ventures. Price, convenience, and service are important, but secondary. If you can't deliver on time and on budget the customer's business suffers, a risk that led to the famous "You can't go wrong buying IBM" mentality. Keep this in mind when preparing revenue projections. It takes time to create a perception that your business will indeed fill orders on time. Some advisors suggest that you back up any projected sales to large companies by six to 12 months. You may be able to shorten this time frame by enlisting an ally in the big company, a normal marketing ploy. Still, plan on it taking longer for revenue to develop than you expect—a conservative and prudent approach to forecasting revenues.

Start-ups are inherently risky. Banks don't like risk. Therefore banks don't like to lend money to start-ups. That doesn't mean that you can't get your banker to lend you money for a start-up. If your personal credit history is good and the amount you seek is small, you might be able to get an unsecured loan. The distinction is that the banker will look to you rather than to your business for repayment of the loan. Then there are nonbusiness loans that are commonly used for business purposes. For example, home equity loans can be used for any legal purpose. If you go this route, make sure to get advice from your accountant to avoid unpleasant tax implications in the future if you withdraw funds you have loaned to your venture.

Cleverness is not wisdom.

Euripides

SBA Low doc, microloan, and 7(a) loans are all good sources of start-up funds. The Small Business Administration's Web site (*www.sbaonline.sba.gov*) is the best place to start, as it will give you a great overview of the SBA loan programs. Your next step is to visit the nearest SBA office (if possible) or at the very least find out what banks in your area participate in SBA financing. Do this on the SBA Web site by going to Financing then to Lender Programs then to the list of certified and preferred lenders. You want the preferred lenders (they are more small business friendly, as a rule, than other banks).

Credit cards, given the historically low rates and the ludicrous offers to switch all of your debt to a new

With interest rates heading up, demand for small business loans is leveling off. To attract small business clients, banks are increasing the number of specialty products they offer, including everything from e-commerce consulting and Internet account access to concierge services (Connecticut-based Liberty Bank offers to make travel arrangements for clients). At the same time, loans are being bundled with other financial services, such as payroll and health, life, and auto insurance—offered free or at a reduced cost, providing a de facto discount on the loan. Some banks even throw in free personal checking accounts for the business owner. (*Business Week*, "Pricey Loans—with Perks," February 28, 2000)

Herbert J. Mallet, CEO of Broudy Printing Inc. in Pittsburgh, uses his American Express Card to buy paper and other printing supplies, because he felt constrained by his personal credit cards' $100,000 borrowing limit. "Using the American Express card for these purposes makes sense for me because it's a corporate card with effectively no limit," Mallet says. "I always pay this bill off entirely at the end of the month. But using the credit card gives me up to 50 days of free financing. If you're talking about a $200,000 purchase of paper, that's a big float. And I save even more money because I discount my supplier bills by 2 to 3 percent, since I'm paying them within 30 days." (*Inc.*, April 2000, p. 118)

card, make attractive alternative financing sources. This can become a very expensive form of debt if you aren't careful. A 2 percent discount for money you repay in 30 days works out to 24 percent per year, scarcely a bargain, and if you don't repay it in time you'll be looking at anywhere from 9 to 22 percent on the unpaid balance—and that's in addition to the original discount. No wonder the credit card companies can afford to be generous in their offers!

There is no sin except stupidity.
OSCAR WILDE

Trade credit may be available if you approach your suppliers in a businesslike manner. They want new customers just as much as anyone else, but don't want to be reckless in their credit policies. Treat them with the respect you treat your banker or other outside investors with, and you will secure some credit from them. This may be for a modest amount at first, perhaps no more than extended dating on small orders, but as you develop a history of prompt payment with your vendors you may be able to get a significant amount of your financing this way—not at start-up, though.

Commercial finance companies are a good source of financing for new businesses. Visit *www.scoredelaware.com/financing* for a clear short article on commercial finance companies. (SCORE is shorthand for Service Corps of Retired Executives, another SBA program to visit.) Some familiar commercial finance companies include The Money Store,

CIT Financing, and TransAmerica. Most major banks have a commercial finance company (for example, Fleet Financial Company). Look in the Yellow Pages. These companies are set up to handle more risky loans than banks are comfortable with, and can provide you the capital you need to get into business.

Equipment manufacturers are eager to develop you into a bigger and better customer. If your venture will need a substantial amount of equipment, look into this kind of financing. Suppose you need 10 personal computers and a server to launch your e-business. You could presumably pay $25,000 out of pocket (mainly for the server and licenses) or lease the equipment (small down payment and a fixed monthly payment thereafter) or finance it through a captive finance company. The decision is partly dollars and cents, partly what you can afford, and partly what best suits your business and its prospects. A captive finance company is one owned by the manufacturer. They can take more of a risk than other lenders, but have to charge for it.

If a man look sharply and attentively,
he shall see Fortune;
for though she is blind,
she is not invisible.

FRANCIS BACON

Gateway's eBusiness Accelerator Leasing program will lease up to $1 million in computing gear and services to new Internet companies that have at least one round of funding. Gateway explains that many customers in this niche don't fit the conservative standards, such as having been in business for two or three years. To decide whether a company gets financing—and how much—Gateway will take a look at the company's executive team, funding, and financial performance. In some cases, Gateway may make getting a stake in the company a condition of lending. The program is more lenient than Compaq Computer's, because there are no membership fees or commitments to a particular platform. (*New York Times*, "Gateway Expands Lease Program for Start-ups," July 28, 2000)

2

What Do You Need the Money For? How Much? When?

The three basic questions of all financing proposals are: What do you need the money for, how much do you need, and when do you need it.

The purpose of the investment drives the type and source of the investment. The need for start-up cash is different from the frantic rush to meet payroll or making a calm decision to expand into a new market. Some of the more common purposes for financing and their sources include the following:

- *Starting a business*: Equity from the owner, investment from three Fs (friends, family, fools) or perhaps an outside investor, loans from the Small Business Administration (SBA) and other government agencies, credit cards, payout from an early retirement.
- *Acquiring inventory*: Cash from operations, terms, and dating from suppliers.
- *Purchasing equipment*: A loan from an equipment manufacturer or bank, payment made to a credit card or finance company; or a business owner may decide to lease instead of purchase.
- *Expanding a business*: Cash from cash flow and operating profits, new equity, a medium- to long-term bank loan to be repaid from

Twin brothers Jason and Judson Keen were passionate about their plan for an e-commerce company called Varyex.com. They hoped to start as an online exchange for used college textbooks and eventually become a link for customers of local grocery stores and other merchants. They approached a speaker at a Birmingham, Alabama, venture-capital group lunch they occasionally attended in their quest for contacts. Clayton McWhorter of Nashville was intrigued and asked them to present their business plan to his private investment group, which later committed $50,000 in seed money to the Keens. (*Kiplinger's Personal Finance* magazine, September 1999, pp. 127–128)

profit, risk capital, proceeds from retirement funds (under some circumstances).

- *Acquiring another business*: Funding from direct investment, a bank loan, cash flow of the acquired entity, seller financing.
- *Paying normal business bills*: Cash from operations, secured credit from a bank, warehouse financing, or funds from a factor or finance company.
- *Increasing working capital*: Stretching payables; funds from new equity, a long-term bank loan, or operating profits.
- *Meeting unexpected personal financial needs of owner*: Personal savings, personal loans, credit cards, a loan from the business, a salary advance.
- *Acquiring fixed assets*: Funds from a mortgage, a long-term debt, seller financing.
- *Unanticipated disaster:* Proceeds from an insurance policy, retained earnings, owner's assets.

What are you planning to buy with the proceeds? Although it may sound odd, many small business owners raise money (or try to) before thinking their needs through. If you don't know what you need and why you need it, you can't defend your plan, nor present a cogent argument to financing sources.

What do you really need? Look at what you think you need from three points of view: bare bones, most likely, and what you'd get if money were no object. Keep in mind that ultimately any acquisition has to be paid for out of operating profits. Impulsive purchases destroy budgets. Moreover, bankers look askance at furnishings and equipment that seem to indicate lack of proper business restraint. The less you spend on frivolities, the more you'll have for necessities!

Without money, without hands.
UKRAINIAN PROVERB

Finally, you have to decide whether you can afford the financing. Is this the right time to take on more debt? If capital costs 14 percent (interest rate), and the company earns 5 percent on sales after taxes, how great an increase in sales is required to service a term loan of $10,000? Can the company achieve or exceed that increase? A term loan of $10,000 at 14 percent annual interest amortized over five years costs $232 per month, or $2,784 per year to service. Annual sales would have to increase $55,680 to cover this amount. Is the addition of the equipment purchased by the loan practical? Or is it not going to have that impact on sales?

A side point: The new equipment may increase productivity and profitability, may be necessary so that the business remains competitive, or may represent an expansion of the market for the company (and so on). No financial decision should be made in isolation of such factors—nor should a borrowing decision be made without at least considering the impact of the loan on sales and profits.

What is the timing? Another way to pare down loan costs is to pay close attention to the timing of the disbursement of the loan proceeds. If a loan can be postponed, it may result in lowered costs.

Joe Elizondo, CEO of C.V. Date Company, which processes, packages, and distributes dates, needed flexible sources of credit. "We needed the financing to help us purchase our product from growers and cover our operating expenses during those periods when revenues aren't coming into the company," he explained. With the help of a private investment banker who focused on small, growing companies, C.V. Date was able to put together a package of working-capital financing of various amounts, depending upon where the company was in its cash-flow cycle. The package included vendor financing, accounts-receivable financing, and some equipment leasing. (*Inc.*, March 1999, p. 45)

How will it make your business more profitable? Why does the loan make good business sense? The supporting (and counter) arguments should be jotted down to make sure that good decisions are made more often than not. It's easy to forget why a decision was made months after it was made. The planning process helps you to avoid repeating poor decisions—and makes it easier to repeat good ones.

Money is better than poverty, if only for financial reasons.
WOODY ALLEN

As the old adage goes, "Well begun is half-finished." If you start your business out on the right foot—which means with enough capital to get it up and running without being pinched for cash—your chances of success soar. Part of the puzzle involves start-up costs for initial inventories, leasehold improvements, licenses, and all the other one-time costs that you will incur when you start up your business.

You can hold some of these costs down by using secondhand or borrowed equipment, renting space, and leasing equipment instead of purchasing. But the total amount will probably be more than you expect. Don't underestimate what you might need.

Put your shoulder to the wheel.
AESOP

The dangers of undercapitalization cannot be too strongly emphasized. Get the real figures. If they are manageable, great. If not, perhaps you can find ways to lower them. Don't plow ahead until you are pretty sure that you can afford to go into business.

Use your cash-flow projections to determine how much capital you really need. Look for the deepest cumulative cash-flow negative point. A rough rule of thumb is to double this amount to determine approximately how much capital your venture needs.

Lack of money is the root of all evil.
GEORGE BERNARD SHAW

It is important to be accurate and descriptive and to use vendor sources rather than guesstimates for start-up costs.

The process of going over start-up costs again and again, looking for economies and ways to lower those costs, is excellent practice for actually running your business. Careful cash management is one of those business skills that spells the difference between success and failure.

You will be very accurate in projecting start-up costs if you speak with vendors, check out catalogues and price lists, and look for hard (as opposed to approximate) prices. Don't guess. A businesslike listing of assets will help you build credibility, especially if you can show that you have indeed done everything reasonable to hold costs down.

Accuracy also pays off when you sit down with your banker and explain why you need to borrow

Danny Meyer is a Manhattan restaurateur who hit it big with Union Square Café in 1985 and Gramercy Tavern in 1993. He raised more than $1.5 million from individual investors toward the total $7 million cost of building both the lively, Indian-inspired Tabla and, right next door, Eleven Madison, which echoes turn-of-the-century New York and offers airy views of Madison Square Park. But not everyone is as successful as Meyer has been. Up to 80 percent of restaurants fail or change hands in their first three years. The most common error: Restaurants undercapitalize, go way over budget, and open without enough cash to make payroll, says Gary Levy, an accountant for 150 restaurants, including all of Meyer's. (*Forbes*, October 18, 1999, pp. 117–119)

money for your start-up. That portion of the start-up costs you pay for personally will show up as part of your investment in the business and can on occasion be used as collateral for a loan. Facts impress bankers. Guesses do not.

Use the form called "Start-up Costs You Only Have to Pay Once" in Appendix One to organize your start-up costs. Not all items will apply, and you may have to add others. See the examples.

Remember that you can't run a business without cash. Working capital is defined as current assets minus current liabilities—but for now, you can estimate working capital plus contingency needs to equal the costs of running the business for two months. See Appendix One, "Estimated Monthly Costs," to calculate your monthly figure. Multiply that by three. This figure will provide the (minimum) cushion you need to run the business until it generates revenues and becomes self-supporting.

Ah, take the cash in hand and waive the rest;
Oh, the brave music of a distant drum!
EDWARD FITZGERALD,
THE RUBÁIYÁT OF OMAR KHAYYÁM

You can't run your business successfully without a budget. Nobody can. Cash is slippery and costs rise unless closely watched. You can't borrow money from a bank, secure trade credit, or attract investors without a budget.

Your operating budget serves a variety of purposes. It helps you hold down spending, provides and supports financial self-discipline, and helps you set time-lines and measurable goals. It gives you a scorecard, a way of seeing how well you are doing and whether or not you need to change some business behaviors.

You don't have to become an accountant to understand and use a budget. In fact, you are already familiar with budgeting from handling your personal finances. All your operating budget does is set down the expected amounts and timing of revenues and expenses in a standard form that can be used to strengthen your business decisions. Your operating budget allows you to know *when* you need financing—and when you don't.

> *No horse gets anywhere until he is harnessed.*
> *No steam or gas ever drives anything until it is confined.*
> *No Niagara is ever turned into light and power*
> *until it is tunneled.*
> *No life ever grows great until it is*
> *focused, dedicated, disciplined.*
> Harry Emerson Fosdick, D.D.

Make sure to establish the appropriate time frame for your operating budget. Operating budgets cover a period of time, usually a fiscal year (required for tax purposes), but are most useful if broken down to a monthly or even weekly basis.

Most businesses will find that a monthly budget is the most useful, as it allows enough time to smooth out some of the bumps, yet is short enough so that if you find something going wrong (or going better than you expected) you can take timely action. Information

Nordstrom has been trying to cut costs to boost profits, while maintaining its legendary customer service. Although its sales per square foot of store are the envy of the retailing industry, inefficient opera-tions have prevented Nord-strom's higher sales from boosting its bottom line. For instance, some stores were built too big in recent years. The company has been slashing inventories, reducing its merchandise-buying staff, and using its muscle to extract better prices from suppliers and lower rents from mall land-lords. (*Wall Street Journal*, April 8, 1999, p. B4)

Robert Wehe, former successful banker turned hotel entrepreneur, received a letter from SierraWest Bank offering great terms to refinance the debt on his Meadowmont Lodge in Arnold, California. He investigated a bit, and then jumped at the deal. He refinanced $200,000 in debt and got $175,000 in cash to buy an additional hotel. His new monthly payment, however, came out only slightly higher than the one on his old loan. The terms brought down his interest rate from 11 percent to 8.9 percent. He also replaced a floating rate with a 20-year fixed rate, letting him escape a pending balloon payment when he refinanced earlier. Best of all is that he can sell the hotel more easily in a few years because the loan is assumable. (*Business Week*, "A Jump-Start for Cheap Loans," September 13, 1999)

that is 12 months old can arrive too late to do you much good, especially during the early months of a start-up when reliable patterns haven't been established.

Next, determine how much you really need. Bankers and other investors look with justifiable skepticism at unsubstantiated requests for funds. Try to determine how much you *really* need as opposed to what you think would be nice to have. What is the least you can get by with? Do you have a compelling argument for more money—in terms of added growth, profits, lessened risk, and so forth?

Your financing proposal should make clear:

- How much money you want
- What you want it for
- What kind of money you are seeking (debt or equity)
- When you want it
- Why it will make your business better
- How you'll pay it back
- What your contingency plans might be just in case things don't work out

---

Gold that's put to use more gold begets.
                              WILLIAM SHAKESPEARE

Make a capital equipment list and keep it up to date. Capital equipment are depreciable items that the business will use up over a period of a year or more. Maintaining an updated capital equipment list is useful for insurance as well as tax and inventory purposes, and can make the difference between a "yes" and a "no" on a credit application. Banks and other funding sources (trade, SBA, investors) look to collateral as a comfort factor. If you can provide a clean, up-to-date capital equipment list to substantiate your collateral claims, it gives these people a warm, friendly feeling about your business.

Use your cash-flow budget to carefully manage your cash. There are only four sources of cash: net from operations, new debt, sale of fixed assets, and new investment. That's it. No others allowed. Cash gushes out in innumerable ways, though many are really part of net from operations. In fact, the only dependable and lasting source is from operations. If net from operations continues to be negative, you can only sell off so many assets before you can't continue to be in business. If it looks like it will be negative, new debt or new equity will be hard to come by; investors and bankers aren't fools. Or won't be for long.

It all comes down to cash from operations. The reason for a cash-flow budget is to control the outflow of cash, to make sure that the cash you do spend is used for business reasons that fit in with your business plan. The discipline involved here is tremendous: Operating expenses can be controlled. Profits are tied to operating expenses—"A penny saved is a penny earned"—in the most direct ways. You cannot place too much stress on maximizing operations net.

"If the 1980s had a universal lesson to teach, it is that *cash really is king*—Engelhard's fifth financial principle. This doesn't mean cash in the strict sense of money in the bank, but the ability of a business to throw off enough cash over time through income, depreciation and good working capital management so that it can be sensibly reinvested in the operation. The result of this strategy is a business with solid earnings growth, a business which, in essence, feeds itself." (Engelhard Corporation 1989 Annual Report)

> From birth to 18 a girl needs good parents.
> From 18 to 35, she needs good looks.
> From 35 to 55, good personality.
> From 55 on, she needs good cash.
> SOPHIE TUCKER

3

Where Do You Find Capital for Your Business?

Where and if you can find capital for your business depend on a number of factors. Owners of start-ups most frequently rely on personal assets. Going concerns might look to cash flow, receivables financing, or other business-related sources. Bank financing may hinge on the owners putting in additional cash. A rapidly growing business may choose to sell equity to raise capital.

Every business investor we have ever met wants to be sure that the applicants are more committed to their business venture than they are. Therefore they insist that you invest fully in your business before they reach into their pockets.

What does this mean for you? You have to put your personal assets on the line. You can't hide assets in your spouse's name either. (Well, you can if you are foolish. Most savvy investors look beyond the obvious.)

You may be surprised at the amount of capital you have amassed over the years. Cash (whether in checking or savings accounts or CDs) is the first source. Securities, including stocks, bonds, and mutual funds, are also liquid. Funds invested through an IRA or 401(k) (to $50,000) may be used to finance your business—check with your accountant and attorney first, though, as there are likely to be tax penalties. You may have cash values built up in life insurance policies, which may be borrowed at favorable terms.

Look at the possibilities of refinancing personal credit. While this is primarily a cash flow trick, you may find that you can spring some cash for your venture. Home-equity loans are one form of refinancing. You can weigh the costs of a home-equity loan against the costs of remortgaging your home; both have tax implications. Sell or borrow against assets that you own free and clear. That antique chair you don't dare sit on or your great-grandmother's silverware moldering in the safe deposit box might be put to better use.

Don't forget credit cards as a low-cost source of funds. We receive offers every day urging us to borrow at extraordinarily low rates. More than one business has financed itself through judicious use of credit cards. According to *Business Week*, 50 percent of small business owners surveyed used business credit cards to finance some aspect of their business in 2000. The reason? Small businesses are doing more of their purchasing on the Internet, where plastic is the preferred currency. And then there are perks like cash-back awards and coveted frequent-flier miles.

The point is simple: If you won't invest in your own business, why should anyone else? Your money has to be the first in and the last out.

A business with an income at its heels
Furnishes always oil for its wheels.
WILLIAM COWPER

Don't be shy about asking friends and family for money for your venture. Phil Baker, principal in an informal group of equity investors, always asks people if they have asked their friends, family members, and wealthy acquaintances to invest in their business. If the answer is yes, Phil continues the conversation. If the answer is no, a chilly silence pervades the room. It doesn't matter how good the business model is, or how skilled the management. If the principals have so little confidence in the safety and potential returns of their investment that they haven't invited the three Fs (friends, family, and fools) to get in early, why should they expect a stranger, a professional investor at that, to invest?

> UPS (United Parcel Service), the parcel delivery service whose revenue in 1999 was $27 billion, was started in 1907 when founder Jim Casey borrowed $100 from a friend. (*Forbes*, January 10, 2000, p. 82)

The holy passion of friendship is of so sweet and steady and loyal and enduring a nature that it will last through a whole lifetime, if not asked to lend money.
MARK TWAIN

Look to operating profit as the primary source of expansion capital. In a general way, if you aren't pressed for time, operating profit is the least expensive capital. Cash flow is a short-term source of cash but, if your business is growing, is not a sustainable source. Cash flow and profits go in different directions when a business grows—hence the need for additional capital.

Pay attention to sustaining profits for these reasons:

- *A track record of profitability*, evidenced by growth in retained earnings over several years, makes lenders and other investors more likely to invest in your business.

- *Growing retained earnings* dramatically increases the value of the business. If you decide to sell, do so while retained earnings are going up.
- *Profits and cash flow tend to support each other* in the long run. Short-term, they conflict.

Don't count on increased sales to pull you out of a capital gap. If you know how long your operating cycle is, you can figure out how long it will take you to convert sales into cash. Chances are it will take longer than you think. Once a sale is made and a receivable is generated and finally collected, you may be looking at a period of months. If you, like most businesses, operate with a modest profit as a percentage of sales, the amount of profit left over to ease your capital needs will be small.

The two most beautiful words in the English language are "Check enclosed."

DOROTHY PARKER

There may be times when it makes sense for you to lend your business money, but do so with caution. Make sure to have a legal contract with a stipulated rate of interest (which must be paid) in order to keep the IRS happy.

Why put money in for a short term? There may be personal reasons, such as a looming college tuition bill. There may be tax reasons: principal repayments are not taxable (interest is), and you want to make sure that you don't pay extra when you take the money out of the business. The business need may be predictably short-term, or the business may be tapped out of traditional credit sources.

Loans from officers and owners may have to be subordinated to other debt. Your banker wants to be paid before you take your money out. Subsequent investors will look askance at unsubordinated debt and may request special consideration. If the sums are modest there may be no problem—but if the sum is significant, be prepared to be challenged.

A pro forma balance sheet is used to show the impact of major investments or other financial changes on the condition of a business. You use it to see what the impact of a refinancing would be on the balance sheet for one big reason: bankers look to the balance sheet to determine debt/worth ratios. If these are out of line with their norms, they won't give you a loan.

A balance sheet is the most basic piece of financial information required for managing a business and for obtaining financing. You have to fill out a balance sheet for many trade suppliers; they want to know whether they can safely extend credit to you. Since better than 90 percent of small business financing comes from banks and trade, this is obviously of major importance.

What will your balance sheets show you? They'll show changes from one period to the next, such as the relationship of current assets to current liabilities, and the relationship of debt load to net worth. For example, the inventory of a retailer just before

CEO Murray Dashe has put new life into specialty retailer Cost Plus, thanks to smart merchandising and stringent cost controls. The Oakland, California–based chain of 98 stores has no long-term debt. Buying cubicles secondhand saved the company $400,000. By staggering inventory counts among the stores—instead of closing them all at once—the chain has been able to recoup $500,000 in lost sales. A stint as CEO of a Los Angeles–based electronics retailer during its bankruptcy taught Dashe to be careful with debt and ruthless about controlling expenses. (*Forbes*, October 18, 1999, p. 144)

Christmas is different from the inventory figure in January. The net worth (or owner's equity) figure is meaningless in some regards. Few businesses are sold at book value (net worth) because so many value judgments are buried or concealed in the balance sheet. On the other hand, banks will not lend into negative net worth businesses without compelling reasons, and strong and secure personal guarantees.

Some of the more obvious value judgments are method of depreciation, concealed market values of fixed assets, replacement costs (and/or reserves for replacement), age and condition of inventory and receivables, values placed on "goodwill" or other assets being amortized, condition of liabilities, and contingent liabilities buried in obscure footnotes.

The value judgments are inevitable, but if they are properly documented (a legal requirement for publicly traded companies), you can understand and mitigate their effect on your decisions. Sharp bankers insist on this kind of documentation.

A financier is a pawnbroker with imagination.
A. W. PINERO

Look carefully at your fixed assets, represented as the sum of the values of all plant and equipment owned by the business.

At another level, managing fixed assets is different in substantial ways from managing current assets. Knowing the age and condition of inventory or receivables is essential knowledge; their value is volatile.

Figuring the value and potential return on fixed assets has increased the ROI (return on investment) of many banks in recent years. Since their headquarters building was worth $150,000,000, would Bank of Boston have been better off selling it and leasing it back, thus getting out of the real estate business and investing the proceeds on their core business operations? You bet it would. (It did.)

ROI is the name of the game. But you have to understand what the ROI is and could be before going for it.

The real price of everything, what everything really costs to the man who wants to acquire it, is the toil and trouble of acquiring it.
ADAM SMITH

You also need to learn contribution analysis and break-even analysis.

Contribution analysis examines each product or service to determine how many cents in each sales dollar are available for meeting the overhead costs of the business in a timely fashion. Sales do not equal profits, and not all sales are equal, no matter what the sales force tells you. You can't do contribution analysis without knowing the break-even. Similar considerations apply to borrowing money, which forces fixed costs up, so you need to ascertain what added sales are required. Same with credit policies: How do you figure out what credit to permit your customers? Break-even analysis plays a major role.

David New needed $50,000 to get his company, Roadside Beverage, to the next level. But banks weren't interested in lending to him, because they said he didn't have any assets. But he did—his golden ticket was the trademark "Root 66" on each bottle of his soft drink. New explained his dilemma to David Martin, CEO and founder of Mosaic Technologies, who consequently developed a software program, called First Dollar, to help banks assess the value of patents, trademarks, and formulas. New received a loan of $300,000, which he used for operating capital and equity for future strategic moves or expansion. (*Inc.*, January 2000, pp. 87–91)

Break-even analysis doesn't take much time, especially with a computer. The calculations are easy; the sticking point usually is deciding whether a given expense is fixed or variable. The easy way to solve this: When in doubt, make it a fixed expense. This is conservative (the higher the total fixed cost, the higher the break-even point). Another simple solution some recommend is to add all the questionable expenses and allot half to fixed, half to variable.

The good news is that once analysis has established the break-even point, you can use it again and again—until you add new expense categories, or sales volume changes dramatically, or prices change.

---

*Happy the man who has been able to know
the reasons for things.*

VIRGIL

Figure break-even on either dollar volume or unit sales. We sometimes call this the "bowls of soup analysis." One of Andy's former clients had a downtown soup and salad restaurant. When the client learned that his break-even was 1,175 bowls of soup per day, it made him really sit up and think. Since his restaurant sat 60 people, this meant he'd have to have 20 turns during the lunch hour, which seemed improbable. (His solution: trim the staff, increase prices, limit the menu, and deliver to neighboring office buildings. It worked.) Calculate break-even in terms of the number of widgets to be sold, hours to be billed, or whatever units apply to your business. It is very illuminating.

Break-even analysis helps spot trends early. A break-even that's too high flags a dangerous business venture—or an unprofitable one. A low break-even can signal a market ripe for competition. Profits come from acting on information before the competition does.

Learn financial language before seeking external financing. Unless you are independently wealthy, you will need to persuade other people—friends, bankers, strangers with money—to provide financing. Your credibility will be enhanced by your ability to communicate with them in their language.

As a business owner you want to attract finance—that is, acquire assets, especially financial assets. To do this you must make your venture appealing to the finance community by giving them reason to believe that they will get a good return at an acceptable risk. "Good" and "acceptable risk" are defined by those from whom you seek financing.

Bankers and other financiers have the financial resources you need to make your business grow. Learn their terms and their values, and your chances of securing the right financing for your business improve.

> *Rule No. 1: Never lose money.*
> *Rule No. 2: Never forget Rule No. 1.*
> WARREN BUFFETT

Ken Thuerbach is a former business owner who's made angel investments and served on the boards of two venture capital funds. His advice to business owners in search of capital is to overdeliver, not over-promise. "People don't realize that the more sophisticated an investor is, the less mileage a business owner will get out of making unrealistic promises," Thuerbach explains. "It's much better to err on the side of caution. What many entrepreneurs don't understand is that investors and lenders always care more about the jockey than about the horse." (*Inc.*, September 1999, p. 109)

Be careful when you take on partners or minority shareholders. We tell our small business clients that partnership, as a legal entity, has all the disadvantages of marriage and none of the benefits. The same goes for taking on minority shareholders. These legal relationships are easy to get into but hard to get loose of should they go sour.

Andy knows this well. He entered a partnership with a banker against the advice of his friends and advisors—and when a third person invested in the partnership the affair ended up with lawyers and unnecessary, painful, and expensive disputes.

If you do take on a partner, look for more than money. Complementary talents, business contacts, similar business goals, and a willingness to compromise rank high on the list of desirable attributes.

In fairness, partnerships (legal or otherwise) can be terrific. But make sure that all parties understand the ground rules. Both of us have enjoyed business partnerships that worked, even when the partnerships dissolved.

Mr. Morgan buys his partners; I grow my own.
ANDREW CARNEGIE

The key to obtaining a good hearing with prospective lenders or investors: Be prepared. Rehearse. Present your business idea to people who can give you an honest, fair, thoughtful response. Most SBA programs urge their clients to do this. Many colleges hold "business plan competitions" in order to expose their students to the rigorous questioning investors like to pursue.

As an example, the New Hampshire Women's Business Center's financing programs require that their clients prepare and present financing proposals to a panel of business professionals. The panel usually includes one or more bankers, private investors, business consultants, and at least two small business owners. Participants over the years are unanimous in their praise of this aspect of the training. The "rehearsal" helps participants better understand what the banks and investors will look for, what questions will be raised, and what kind of answers will be requested. This allows the presenters to make their mistakes—and there are almost always mistakes—in a supportive environment.

One oddity has been noticed with novice presenters: They are shy about asking for money, burying the "ask" in small print. Investors want to know how much you want, what the terms are, how the money will profit them (they want to be paid first), and what you will do if things don't pan out the way you hope.

Choose your bank carefully. One bank in town will handle start-up loans. The others won't. A few banks may be comfortable with restaurant and hospitality businesses that other banks shun. Some banks are very careful in assembling their loan portfolio, and seek a balance between service and retail, manufacturing and hospitality. Any bank can become "loaned up" in one or more categories.

This is important information that you can benefit from—but you have to dig for it. Ask other business

Gene and Janet Maddalena's wholesale cheesecake business had customers across the country, and in Canada and Mexico. But the thriving business had classic cash-flow problems—customers were slow to pay and larger customers squeezed the Maddalenas for discounts. They decided to take on a partner, personally guaranteeing the partner's investment in the business. When the Maddalenas and the partner disagreed on key issues, the partner called in the loans, leaving the Maddalenas on the hook for more than $1 million. They filed for personal bankruptcy, and creditors forced their company into Chapter 7 (liquidation bankruptcy) as well. (*Success*, May 1999, p. 32)

owners, accountants, and financial consultants. Ask your own banker. In Portsmouth, New Hampshire, where Andy lives, two banks (Fleet and Olde Port) aggressively seek small business lending opportunities, while the other banks are less interested in this market. These other banks make a lot of small business loans but have more rigid guidelines. One bank goes so far as to say it doesn't make small business loans but does make loans to small business owners. Figure that one out!

As you shop for a bank, seek SBA-certified lenders. These are lenders who can expedite the SBA process, and are obviously interested in making loans to small businesses.

Local banks tend to be more interested in community businesses than branches of giant banks. Of course there are exceptions, such as Fleet Bank in Portsmouth. Local independent banks are a good place to start, though, as they tend to specialize in the local economy and can usually give quicker answers than bigger, less local banks.

Choose your banker carefully. He or she is more important than the bank.

Your dealings with your bank will always be filtered through the person you deal with—so choose that person carefully. You want to talk with your banker in good times and bad, keeping lines of communication open. While you don't have to be friends with your banker, you do have to trust him or her. Some qualities to look for:

- *Chemistry.* We've all met people we just click with from the start—or can't abide from the git-go. Follow your gut reaction. Your banker will be a confidant, a part of your team. If you don't feel comfortable now, you'll feel less comfortable later.

- *Willingness to learn about your business*. You can pick up on this during your first visit. Will he or she visit your office?
- *Experience*. You can't afford to train a brand-new banker. You can be reasonably sure that any commercial loan officer has some facility with finance, or he or she wouldn't be sitting behind that desk.
- *Experienced and informed backup*. A seasoned branch manager or a more senior loan officer who is willing to keep an eye on your account is a big help.

Creditors have better memories than debtors, and creditors are a superstitious set—great observers of set days and times.

BENJAMIN FRANKLIN

Look for nonbank lenders as well as banks. As noted earlier, about 90 percent of small business financing comes from banks and trade. The remaining 10 percent comes from a variety of nonbank sources. These include:

- Near banks, such as savings and loans, and trust companies
- Consumer finance, sales finance, and commercial finance companies

Holly Hitzemann, owner of Great American Stock, a $1.2 million provider of stock photographs, knows firsthand about the importance of building good relationships with one's financial backers. A local bank financed Hitzemann's Rio Rancho, New Mexico, company throughout much of its growth. When a major new contract stalled during the final negotiations in 1998, Hitzemann began to worry about her company meeting its financial obligations, particularly a balloon payment due in three months. Thanks to her frank and early disclosure of her company's problems, her banker was very supportive. "He worked out a much better refinancing arrangement for us than I would have even asked for," she remembers. (*Inc.*, September 1999, p. 109)

Philip Brach's World Trade Knitting Mills in Brooklyn, New York, makes sweaters for a large national retailer and has annual sales of $10 million. He started factoring his bills in 1985, when a major bank gave him a $1 million credit line at a better interest rate. Six months later the bank rescinded its offer, explaining that World Trade was too big for its small business loans and too small for the financing it offered medium-size firms. Brach went back to factoring and built a relationship with Manhattan-based Quantum Corporate Funding. Factoring has allowed him to increase his production and sales by about 25 percent in two years. (*Success*, May 1999, p. 18)

There is no good in arguing with the inevitable.
The only argument available with an east wind
is to put on your overcoat.
                    JAMES RUSSELL LOWELL

Don't get fooled by the red-hot market for IPOs that made instant billionaires in high-tech businesses in the late 1990s. If your business has the potential for growth that those companies have, you'll be bombarded by offers to take your company public.

Otherwise, forget about it until such time as you do begin to receive feelers from professionals, such as investment bankers and major law firms.

"Look at the money raining down on Silicon Valley and you might think that raising capital is as easy as sending a business plan to a venture capitalist and waiting for the phone to ring. Not quite. There's lots of money, but there are also lots of crappy plans. A name-brand venture capitalist might get 10,000 plans a year and fund only 25." (Guy Kawasaki, CEO of Garage.com, a Palo Alto—based start-up capital company and author of *Rules for Revolutionaries*, as quoted in *Forbes*, January 10, 2000, p. 188)

4

What's the Difference Between a Business Plan and a Financing Proposal?

Your business plan and financing proposal share many elements—even if they are used for different purposes. They both have detailed financial projections based on a set of assumptions that are outlined in the narrative portion of the plan or proposal. They both should make it easy for the reader to understand what the business is, why it will succeed, and how it will pay off an investment in the business.

There are some major differences.

You write the business plan first because it generates the information that will appear in the financing proposal. It includes some information that the proposal does not, such as identification of operational weaknesses and speculations about the future.

Your business plan should be as objective and factual as you can make it. Your own time and money will be invested on the basis of the plan—and surely you don't want to invest either unwisely.

Your financing proposal should be tailored to its audience. This doesn't mean that it should be fiction, but rather that the interests and expectations of the audience will shape the final proposal. A proposal for a banker will stress stability and dependable sources of repayment, while a proposal for an "angel," or private investor, will stress the potentially high payout for the investor should the business thrive.

Every man has a right to his opinion,
but no man has a right to be wrong in his facts.
                                        BERNARD M. BARUCH

Your business needs capital for a variety of reasons. The most common needs for capital are:

- *Start-up capital to get the business going.* This usually comes from your resources, close acquaintances, and in some cases from outside investors.
- *Expansion of a going business.* Growth consumes capital at a rapid pace. Expansion capital usually will be in the form of equity rather than debt.
- *A shot of capital to smooth out the cash flow of an ongoing operation.* This may be handled with a short-term (90 days or less) loan or a line of credit. If the cash shortfalls are sporadic, a line of credit is more flexible than a short-term loan that has to be negotiated each time a small loan is needed.

- *Refinancing a business to attain a better balance of debt and equity.* This is ordinarily a call for new equity but if a company has followed an overly conservative financial pattern, more debt may be helpful to increase revenue and profit.
- *Buying another business.* In most small to mid-size acquisitions, the seller will take back a portion of the selling price as subordinated debt to allow the purchaser to secure bank financing. In 99 percent of acquisitions the buyer has to put down enough equity to meet the bank's criteria, and subordinated debt is frequently a key part of the mix.

Your business plan's cash-flow pro forma, or projection, will identify the amount of capital you need and when you will need it. It will be a key in justifying your financing request. Be realistic: don't inflate or understate the amount you need. You can always ask your banker for his or her advice—the fact that you have a well thought out cash-flow pro forma will make their job easier. (Other investors may be less willing to provide advice.)

You must be prepared to justify your request. What are your assumptions? What are the market conditions? How will you repay the loan or provide a healthy return on equity? In other words: Why do you need their money?

The value of discussing a financing request with your banker is that their job is making sure that your business prospers. They've seen a lot of proposals and have crunched a lot of numbers. Put that set of skills

Douglas Palmer, who works part-time at a lighting store, made a connection between people who purchase lighting for their game rooms and his business plan class. With his partner, Bryce Kumka, they created the Darting Lamp, a dartboard floor lamp. Their business plan won first place in the 1999 Enterprise Creation Competition, a business plan contest sponsored by Ball State University in Muncie, Indiana, and Miami University in Oxford, Ohio. Competition judges were impressed with the partners' preparation and presentation. "In their presentation," a judge said, "they answered all the questions you would raise if you were considering investing money in their idea." (*Entrepreneur,* "Bull's Eye," July 1999)

to work for you—and be prepared to revise your request if their logic is compelling.

Money is a kind of poetry.
WALLACE STEVENS

There is no one single "best" format for a business plan or financing proposal. We have our favorite, but one size does not fit (and cannot fit) all businesses. Make sure if you must use a computerized business plan/financing proposal, that the format to which it will constrict your proposal really fits your business. Chances are good that it won't.

Almost all plans and proposals contain the following elements:

- Cover sheet, showing the business address, phone, fax, and e-mail
- Table of contents
- Overview or executive statement
- Description of the business, its markets and products, competition, marketing, and operations plans
- Detailed financial statements including balance sheets and income and cash-flow statements
- Supporting data, including tax records and contracts

The section describing the business is the most involved and takes far longer than any other part of the plan or proposal. Don't be surprised if 80 percent or more of your planning time is spent on this section. Some of its common components are:

Executive statement, providing a brief statement (one page or less) of what the business is expecting from the plan and why it represents a good investment. This is usually written last, after the plan is complete (including the financials).

Business description, which lays out the business's history and structure, its place on the business lifecycle, and information about the industry.

Product or service (or combination) description.

Market analysis. This is the core of your plan, and the part that will take the most intense thought and research to adequately complete. In this part you identify your prospect and customers; define what strategies you will use to position your business and distinguish it from its many competitors; and spell out what is unique and notable about your products, service, and business operation. This part includes information about your location (or locations), distribution channels, and promotional plans. The key here is your understanding of your competitors, both direct and indirect. You cannot effectively position your business without knowing both your markets' perceptions of your business and the competition.

SWOT (Strengths, Weaknesses, Opportunities, Threats) analysis. An increasingly important piece of the plan is a section devoted to opportunities (and strategies to maximize them) as well as

Just two years out of Yale, 23-year-old James Prosek earned close to $220,000 as an artist and author of several books. His first, *Trout: An Illustrated History*, sold more than 60,000 copies while *The Complete Angler* was dubbed "eloquent and life affirming" by eminent literary critic Harold Bloom. Prosek's sister Jennifer, a savvy entrepreneur and part owner of a PR firm, wants to help her brother preserve the creative, unharried life to which he is accustomed. She is helping him implement a 67-page business plan, which states his objective to be recognized as a serious author and painter, spells out revenue and profit goals for three years down the road, and elaborates on personnel and board structure. (*Inc.*, "Brand in the Making," October 1999)

threats (and strategies to minimize them). Many lenders turn to this first, since it shows at a glance how deeply you have thought about your strategies for the coming year or years.

Key players. Your plan should identify key players, especially the management, and also outside advisors such as board members and professional advisors. Key player resumes live in the appendix. A personnel plan is needed—how many employees, hired at what times, with what kind of qualification or training?

Contingency plans ("Plans B and C") are useful. What will you do if business falls flat, or if it grows dramatically? Investors are always interested in such contingency planning and may use it as a key measure of your management ability.

*Business is never so healthy as when, like a chicken,
it must do a certain amount of scratching for what it gets.*
HENRY FORD

We've put together this list of 10 Common Questions about business plans and some answers.

1. *Why write a business plan?* The best reason is to better understand your business. The planning process will help you root out assumptions about your business, find areas where information will help you make better decisions, and identify weaknesses and strengths so you can act accordingly. This is great insurance.

Secondary reasons are to please bankers, secure investments, woo employees, persuade suppliers to extend credit to you, and (a general but important point) to communicate clearly with all of your stakeholders.

2. *How should I use my business plan?* You will use it as a guide to the future, as a way to establish realistic goals and objectives, set benchmarks and go/no go points, and communicate to the entire company what goals are important. You *can* use it as the basis of a financing proposal, and probably will.

3. *How long does it take to write a plan?* The answer to this is ambiguous: it depends. You can write a first draft in several hours, polish it up, and prepare a first cut at the financials over a weekend. Most of us take a long time sharpening our pencils and postponing the planning—that's why it seems to take such a long time.

Once your first draft is put together in a three-ring binder, it can take weeks to make it useful. If you already have detailed, factual information about your markets, their perceptions of what values you present them, and how they think you stack up against your competition, this may be a matter of a day or two. However, most of us do not have such information, and getting it takes time and thought.

A rule of thumb: the more information you have before starting the planning process, the shorter the time assembling an excellent plan will be.

Marian Fletcher, who runs a profitable party-planning and catering business in Baltimore, didn't know what she was doing when she began working on her business plan. She got some library books and a booklet from the Department of Economics' Division of Business Development, which provided useful demographic information. She also enrolled in Women Entrepreneurs of Baltimore City (WEB), a local entrepreneurial education program where she received invaluable feedback on early business plan drafts. Fletcher says she referred to her plan extensively during the first few months in business and has since revised it. "I found I could get my products cheaper and more easily, and I learned that it would take me twice as long to train new employees than I initially thought it would," she explains. (*Business Start-Ups Online*, "Compose a Winning Business Plan," 2000 issue)

Where is the wisdom we have lost in knowledge?
Where is the knowledge we have lost in information?
T. S. ELIOT

4. *How many pages should my plan be?* We have seen a great plan in six pages, and rotten plans that weigh more than a small car. It must be long enough to explain the business opportunity and how you will capitalize on it, but short enough to be understood. If the plan is too complex it won't communicate well.

5. *How much detail is necessary?* Be careful not to lapse into fun with numbers (too much trivia in the financials gets in the way)—but provide enough detail to answer key questions about the business opportunity you are attempting to benefit from. This will vary from one business to another.

6. *Who should be involved in the planning process?* We are great fans of driving the plan as far down into the business as you can. People on the front lines know more than you may credit them with knowing, and if they are involved in the planning process, they tend to buy into it better than if the plan is driven from the top down.

7. *Can my accountant write it for me?* Sure, if you want it to be his or her plan. You should avail yourself of your accountant's help in translating the conceptual material (the first major section) into financial formats. But the thinking and underpinning of those numbers has to

come from you and your colleagues. Otherwise you will surely find yourself stammering, red-faced and ignorant, when your banker asks why will sales be higher next year, or cash flow weak in the fourth quarter, or growth so costly.

I thatched my roof when the sun was shining, and now I am not afraid of the storm.
GEORGE F. STIVERS

---

8. *How can I get information for a start-up?* If you can find a business similar to the one you want to start, ask them for information. If it is non-competitive with you (serving a different trading area, for example) the owner may be willing to share information. Bankers, consultants, faculty members of business schools, Small Business Development Centers, suppliers, and other interested parties may put you in touch with other start-ups, as well as refer you to secondary sources such as Robert Morris or Financial Information of America.

Trade associations are especially helpful. The Gale *Dictionary of Trade Associations* lists more than 30,000 trade associations in the United States. One or more will be close to what you propose. Call those associations and ask for help.

Gale also publishes *The Small Business Sourcebook*, which provides detailed information on more than 400 small businesses. Your library probably has both of these wonderful resources.

If you'd like help writing your business plan, you can hire a professional business plan writer. Just make sure he or she has a general business background and is familiar with such areas as accounting, bookkeeping, and marketing. He or she should also be acquainted with financial statements, business jargon, and your local business community. Ask for references and writing samples, if possible. Both of us have written business plans for clients. Our fees have varied, depending on the amount of research and analysis we have to do. A great resource for learning more about business plans is Andy's *Business Planning Guide* (Upstart Publishing), which has sold more than 500,000 copies and was named by *Forbes* magazine as the best book on the subject for small businesses.

"A business plan is not a miraculous conception. In order to write one, you need to be able to answer a lot of very tough questions that are typically based upon the history of your business, and its current operations and business prospects. Any investor or lender would want a business plan to clearly demonstrate what the owner plans to do, how he'll create profits for himself and his investors and what his strategy is for paying off any debt he incurs along the way." (Chris Mercer, CEO of Mercer Capital in Memphis, Tennessee, as quoted in *Inc.*, "Who Can Help Out with a Business Plan?" June, 1, 1999)

Go online. The Internet provides a forum for many small business owners, especially through sites provided by business publishers, trade associations, and suppliers ranging from Apple to Zenith.

9. *How accurate do forecasts and pro formas have to be?* There is no set percentage, but you will increase your ability to forecast with experience. Fixed expenses such as rent and insurance payments and salaries and benefits are highly predictable, say 95 percent for the coming year. Variable expenses, which rise or fall with sales, are less easy to forecast, as sales forecasts are notoriously erratic. If you hit 85 percent, you are doing a good job. If you create a range of sales forecasts (high, low, most likely) and use this as the basis for your variable expenses, you will not only be more accurate but also will be building up material for a set of contingency plans.

10. *Where can I get financial information?* The same places as a start-up (see question 8) but with a huge additional source: your historical financial statements. These help you spot trends and seasonal patterns. Over time the changes between one set of statements and the next will become the foundation of your financial management.

A banker is a fellow who lends you his umbrella when the sun is shining and wants it back the minute it begins to rain.
MARK TWAIN

SECTION II:

Getting Money for
Your Business

5

What Are Investors' Special Concerns for Financing Going Businesses?

Going businesses need to pay attention to their "business model"—the way they plan to make money going forward—fully as much as start-ups do. How will you make more money with this injection of capital? Will the strategies that worked well in the past continue to work in the near future? This is particularly important in this e-business world, where so much is changing rapidly. Retailers have to understand that the Internet will affect their business. Two Web sites, *www.seacoastonline.com* and *www.seacoastnh.com*, provide many examples of restaurants and other businesses turning the Web to their advantage.

Be clear on the risks and opportunities that your venture faces. Investors like to see these risks and opportunities spelled out in your plan. It shows them that you have your eyes open, have thought carefully about how to deal with them, and won't just be reacting if and when the risks or opportunities pop up.

Your "burn rate" is a measure of how fast you are burning up capital. Serious investors are keen on knowing this; it makes a major difference to their assessment of the risk involved in providing another round of financing. Companies experiencing rapid growth often run out of cash before operating profits come rolling in. If you are in this dangerous but exciting phase, ask your accountant or treasurer to measure this. Once you know what you face, you (and your investors) can do something about it.

Whatever you have, you must either use or lose.
HENRY FORD

How does Dun & Bradstreet rate your business? You need to know how your suppliers and other creditors view your business, and the odds are this is one source they all use. Check your business credit history. Is the information up-to-date and accurate? Visit D&B's Web site, *www.dnb.com*, a good example of an old-economy business that is learning to use the Internet to its advantage. As D&B's Web site points out, seven out of 10 small businesses have access to the Net.

Advocating honesty in all your financial dealings may seem too trite to be useful, but trust and credibility lie at the heart of every financing decision. Nobody wants to deal with shady people who trim the truth to suit their present need. Be honest with your banker. Be open and forthcoming—no redefining what "is" is. Concealing a problem that your banker (or other investors) should be aware of is foolish, as their expertise in solving problems goes along with their money. Or should. Disingenuousness is just another way to tell a lie, and will shatter your credibility in the future.

Don't be cross if your banker turns your loan application down or an investor declines the chance to put some capital into your business. These are business decisions made on grounds that you want to be aware of. Rage won't help. Instead, ask what tipped their decision. Listen carefully and don't be defensive—you may well learn something that will help you.

Cosigners can help repair a shaky credit history. Andy cosigned for a friend whose business was shy of capital, thus making normal financing available. The criteria cosigners heed are informal: trust in the individual rather than the business, and have the capacity to absorb a loss if need be. As it happened, Andy's cosigning provided just enough leverage for the business to make it to the next level and become bankable by itself. Very satisfying.

A record of profitability makes it much easier to secure financing. Investors expect the future to follow past performance (within limits). They look at past and current profits as indicators that their investment will be secure. Your tax returns and audited financials will make the case that you have indeed been profitable—no doubt about it. More than one small business owner has made the error of underreporting income (a.k.a. tax fraud) in the mistaken belief that when it will be to their advantage to show a strong profit history their unsupported word will suffice to mollify skeptics. It won't. Aside from the very real possibility of incurring IRS wrath, such chicanery will cost dearly when it is time to sell the business.

When he needed money to expand his profitable and growing printing company in order to provide order fulfillment and printing services for Internet companies, John Ferretti didn't ask just anyone. He contacted prospects he knew through Early Stage East, a two-day event he cofounded in Delaware to bring together entrepreneurs, venture capitalists, and investors. "My involvement in Early Stage East made it possible for me to start building some important relationships and to have a lot of conversations about my company and my business plan," Ferretti explains. His company received $50,000 from an angel investor and a $150,000 seed-capital infusion from an early-stage venture-capital firm. (Inc., April 2000, p. 117)

As dot.com mania expands far beyond its Silicon Valley origins, entrepreneurs and investors in more than 80 cities around the world gather at fashionable watering holes on the first Tuesday evening of every month. Entrepreneurs are identified by the green dots on their nametags, investors by red dots. Hobnobs have yellow dots on their nametags, in case they later want to become greens or reds. However, as a result of the technology stock meltdown in April 2000, investors are becoming more selective about what venture capitalists they want to give money to. (New York Times, "Red Dot, Meet Green: If It's Tuesday Network!" July 16, 2000)

"Know thyself" is a good saying, but not in all situations. In many it is better to say "Know others."
MENANDER

Bull markets are a good time to seek financing. Whether the route is through angel investors, venture capitalists, private placements, or even an IPO, money flows more readily when the stock market is surging. However, such markets don't continue forever, so timing becomes critically important. The first eight months of 2000 showed what happens when the market has a major correction. IPOs are harder to place, venture capitalists become more picky, and bankers begin to tighten up their underwriting criteria.

Keep a weather eye open for changes in the economy. Is the state of the economy good? Are economic trends positive? This is easy to track. Visit *www.fool.com* or *www.quicken.excite.com* or any similar Web site. These sites provide up-to-date, understandable, and reliable economic news. They have to; that's how they stay in business. Politics affects financing. Think of the SBA (*www.sbaonline.sba.gov*). Their programs reflect past political orthodoxies: programs for women, minorities, veterans, economically displaced workers. You name it, there's a program aimed at it.

The most effective way to cope with change is to help create it.
I. W. LYNETT

Election years, especially presidential elections, can cause the stock market to worry about change. State and local politics, where decisions about roads, zoning, taxes, and similar matters are made, can be the most important factor for some industries. Make a living selling crushed rock or cement or heavy equipment to companies that build highways? (This is why lobbyists abound. A staggering percentage of the national economy is based on government purchases.)

It helps to be in a hot industry if you are seeking substantial amounts of financing. Hot industries such as communications, biotech, and genetic research and mapping (and suppliers to these industries) find it easier to secure cash than, say, e-tailers, which were 1999's hot industry. In 2000, DNA (the genetic stuff) is extremely enticing to the investment community. Pharmaceuticals are heating up as the population ages, but they face a lot of political challenges.

---

*I have not observed men's honesty
to increase with their riches.*
THOMAS JEFFERSON

Prisms break light into its component colors, providing a better understanding of how light works. Take this as a metaphor for any problem solving: break a large problem into its component parts and it is much easier to deal with. Every physics or math student since Aristotle knows this trick. It's just that we sometimes forget it. When applied to financing decisions, this is known as due diligence, a thorough and systematic analysis of all important aspects affecting

With many e-commerce companies suffering zero profits, negative market sentiment, and fleeing investors, there's still one true growth industry: hyping the industry size itself. Eager to woo capital and consumers, some Web companies have been offering up eye-popping estimates of their potential markets. After all, operating in a multibillion-dollar industry tends to be one of the few positives a dot.com can tout. For example, in late 1999 GoodHome.com announced that "decorating and shopping online" for home furnishings was "an estimated $101 billion industry"—a startling claim, considering total online shopping for 1999 amounted to just $20 billion. (*Wall Street Journal*, August 8, 2000, p. A1)

Think outside the U.S.–dollar box. There are many other lenders out there. Turned down by domestic lenders—including the bank they had dealt with for more than 100 years—our friend Pete Worrell, an investment banker, secured a loan from a Dutch bank for a large dairy products company. He tells us that these foreign banks are sometimes willing to take chances that no American bank could or would. How do you find such banks? Ask your banker if there is a financing consultant in your neck of the woods.

the financing of a business. Visit the Web site *www.fsb.com/fortunesb/articles/0,2227,661,00.html* for "your due diligence crib sheet."

Go visual as you think of financing. While linear thinking (step one, step two . . .) is useful, it has limits. Mind mapping is a technique that helps you identify new connections and new ideas about your business (or any other puzzle). Pay a visit to *http://world.std.com/~emagic/mindmap.html*. It provides a great overview of this helpful tool. Stuck on a speech you have to make to your banker? Try mind mapping.

Visit *www.ozemail.com.au/~caveman/Creative/* for an interesting introduction to visual and other nonlinear tools. Visual cues from clip art may help you puzzle through a problem. Remember: One picture is worth a thousand words.

---

*He who can see three days ahead
will be rich for three thousand years.*
JAPANESE PROVERB

Determine the root causes of your need for financing. It won't be the first thing that pops into your mind. Remember the saying "To a hammer, every problem is a nail"? The real causes are not obvious. A cash-flow problem may stem from a flawed personnel policy or other operational area. It may also come from slow collection of receivables, unwise credit extensions, lack of capital, or a host of other financially rooted causes—but these are easily spotted and cured. A financial person looks for financial causes; his or her tools are financial analysis.

Another person might look to slow sales (Aha! Sell more! Drive that top line!) or to lack of marketing. It depends on what tools we are most comfortable with. The way around this is to make sure that you discuss the problem with your board, top managers, even consultants, in order to get to what really is causing the problem. (Hint: financial statements are reports of human activities.)

A successful life is not an easy life.
It is built upon strong qualities,
sacrifice, endeavor, loyalty, integrity.
GRANT D. BRANDON

Rehearse your presentation before making the real presentation to potential investors. Maybe your financing proposal is terrific. Even so, the presentation of that proposal makes a difference. As the owner or president, you will be required to defend the proposal, explain how and why this is a good idea for the investor, answer their questions, provide more details or whatever is necessary to help them understand what the deal is.

What are the terms? That is, what's in it for the investor? State this right up front. It's the first thing investors want to know. Two elements are involved. First is return *of* capital. When will the investors get their investment back? Most venture capitalists want a relatively short horizon, three to five years being normal. Banks want to make sure their depositors' capital is safe but aren't in as much of a rush. Insurance companies have traditionally been very patient,

Doron Aspitz, CEO of Blue Pumpkin Software, decided to call a corporation and persuade it to invest in his company. Blue Pumpkin's software helps companies schedule their customer-service employees, whether they're helping by phone, e-mail, or on line. Aspitz targeted Siemens because of the company's routing engine. He knew someone there who believed in his product. It also helped that Siemens was committed to supporting smaller firms that could strategically enhance its business. (*Entrepreneur*, July 2000, p. 38)

As Greg Garvis's temporary employment service kept growing, so did its cash needs, always just beyond the reach of its internally generated finances. He had to turn down potential sales because he didn't have enough cash to cover the payroll. When he turned to bank loan officers, they demurred. So he turned to friends and appealed to customers for a better turn-around. Three years into running his business, Garvis had paid down all his major obligations and closed the year with $1.5 million in sales. His employees had grown from one to six. Based on so fine a performance, one of his customers—a bank—finally agreed to a $250,000 revolving line of bank credit. (*Inc.*, "Seed Capital: The 12-Step Program," February 1, 1994)

since they look for steady returns on capital over a long period.

Second is return *on* capital. Venture capitalists look for a high rate of return, commensurate with the risk they take and the yield they need to cover other ventures, say 30 to 40 percent IRR (investment rate of return). Banks look for 7 to 12 percent annual returns, but don't take much risk if they can help it. Andy attended an entrepreneurial conference at Cornell University where the panel, led by a very senior Pepsi Cola executive, repeatedly interrupted the otherwise excellent presentations by asking "What's the deal?" You don't want the deal—the terms of the investment—to be a mystery. A rule to follow: State the terms first, then spend the rest of your presentation justifying it in terms of risk, reward, and market details.

Everything yields to diligence.
ANTIPHANES

Have you thoroughly examined to what extent you can self-finance? If you can lower the amount of financing required from outsiders you will lower the cost of capital. Usually operations will be the number-one source (this is where retained earnings comes from), followed by balance sheet items that might be sold, refinanced, or otherwise converted to more profitable use. Bankers would rather see you borrow the amount you really need than too much (which increases risks) or too little (ditto). Shrewd bankers will push you on this.

What is best for people is what they do for themselves.
BENJAMIN FRANKLIN

Think internationally. Think globally. Not just for financing sources, but for operational profits. The Internet has made it possible for a small toy manufacturer in Rollinsford, New Hampshire, to sell products all over the world. Check out *www.kinderworks.com*. Do you think Kinderworks could expand this to the world? Sure they can. And will. While their main marketing and distribution channels are sales representatives and catalogues, the Internet frees them to profitably widen their sales area.

The communications revolution leads to Internet businesses. The B2B (business to business) and B2C (business to consumer) models are well known but somewhat misleading. Perhaps P2P is more apposite: paths to profitability. The Internet and other electronic wonders are tools, not cure-alls, and will be more likely to help you take advantage of new opportunities than to totally change the way you do business. Keep this in mind when seeking financing. The same old rules of commerce still apply. Find customers, make them happy, make profits. E-commerce is an addition to your arsenal of tricks, not a substitute for it.

To the very last he [Napoleon] had a kind of idea;
that, namely, of La carrière ouverte aux talents,
The tools to him that can handle them.
THOMAS CARLYLE

At age 72, Poppy Bridger had decided her time had come. To go into business, that is. The Ph.D. chemist had retired after a 45-year career as a precious-metals specialist at several large laboratories, but the life of leisure bored her. When a small lab came up for sale, Bridger didn't hesitate. She took her $250,000 nest egg to buy the Anaheim Test Laboratory in Santa Ana, California, with her two children cheering her on. Although her savings might have been more safely invested elsewhere, Bridger plans to eventually pass the lab on to her son and daughter. (*Business Week*, "Senior Start-ups," August 14, 2000)

PrintNation.com's core business is online distribution, and it sells ink, paper, and other tools of the trade to commercial printers. By aggregating purchases of its 2,000 members, PrintNation is able to cut better deals with suppliers. And finding bargains is crucial to commercial printers, whose businesses average 3 percent margins. PrintNation's typical order averages $400 per visit, and its discounts run 5 to 10 percent. Ten months after opening its business, PrintNation is selling hundreds of thousands of dollars' worth of products each month. And it has attracted more than $31 million in financing. (*Business Week*, "Printing Money," August 14, 2000)

A carefully chosen board of directors (or advisors) will help make your case to investors. They represent stability and continuity. They provide assurance that a range of opinions have been weighed and evaluated. A board of directors or advisors can take much of the weight off your shoulders, sometimes by making a phone call or a suggestion or a referral. They dramatically widen your scope. You can tap into their networks, learn from their experience, and benefit from their business acumen. The cost to you is minimal—many small business directors and advisors don't want to be paid, while others will go so far as to make a direct investment in your business. Investors know this. It can make the difference between getting the financing you need and not getting it.

6

What Do Bankers Look For?

Except for bank credit-policy reasons or banking law, banks reject applications for small business loans for the following credit-related reasons:

- Poor moral risk (i.e. the applicant is not trustworthy, credit-worthy)
- Too little owner's equity
- Poor earnings record
- Questionable management
- Low-quality collateral
- Slow/past-due trade or loan payment record
- Inadequate accounting system
- Start-up or new company
- Other: Only 4 percent of rejections have other reasons

One form of insurance is to spread the risk. Don't be dependent on one banker. Bankers move, retire, defenestrate, get promoted, leave banking, have squabbles with the loan review committee. Plus, a line of credit may have to be paid out for 90 days each year. If you have two banks, you use both, keep both happy, satisfy the bank examiners, and have surplus credit available if you need it.

Having been a banker, Andy advises all his clients to become familiar with basic bank loan terminology.

Know the kind of credit you need. The basic rule is to fit the term of the loan to the purpose. A real-estate loan will run 15 years or more, and be repaid from operating profits, while an inventory loan is short-term and gets repaid from the inventory turn. Some loans call for term payments, which include principal and interest, others for interest only with lump-sum principal reductions. The package can become complex.

Loans may be *secured* or *unsecured*. The security may be collateral (personal assets, business assets) or a guarantee from a cosigner or in some cases an out-side agency such as the Small Business Administration. Unsecured loans are hard for a new small business to come by, since bankers are risk-averse (see p. 66) and depend on you to repay your loan on time and on term.

Knowledge is the antidote to fear.
RALPH WALDO EMERSON

Term loans are familiar. You borrow a sum and repay it in monthly or other periodic payments. Each payment has principal and interest, with the interest front-loaded just as in a mortgage, where the early payments are primarily interest and the later payments primarily principal. Think of your basic car loan as an example.

Term loans come in three flavors: *short-term* (a year or less), *medium-term* (one to three years), and *long-term* (usually no longer than five to seven years).

Short-term loans are for short-term needs, such as acquiring seasonal inventory or covering a cash-flow gap. If the need is short, so is the loan.

Medium-term loans are usually for equipment that is expected to be used for a term equal to or longer than the loan itself. They can also be used to boost working capital in certain circumstances. In either case, these loans are repaid from operating profits over the period of the loan. *Working-capital loans* are often tied to an investment of additional capital.

Long-term loans range from heavy equipment to fixed-asset acquisition, such as real estate, and may go as long as 15 years. The term limits vary from one bank to another. Like medium-term loans, these are usually repaid from operating profits.

Lines of credit are more flexible. These allow you to make interest-only payments, paying the principal down as you can. Most lines of credit require an annual period when the loan is repaid in full for 30 or 60 days in order to avoid "evergreen" loans that put the bank in an invidious position.

Bankers have other loan instruments, but for most small businesses these are unnecessary. A letter of credit from the international department of a major bank, for example, will only be needed if you do business abroad.

As part of their plan for growth, Susan Ernst and her husband acquired Royal Electric Construction Corporation, an electrical and telecommunications contractor in Columbus, Ohio. To help them cover operating expenses, they approached two banks for a line of credit. The large national bank didn't seem too interested, but Commerce National Bank, a local bank specializing in serving small businesses, was. Getting loan approval was easy—within one week of their meeting Ernst heard that funds were available and learned the specifics of the bank's terms. (*Inc.*, April 2000, p. 118)

And in the seat to faith assigned,
Where ask is have, where seek is find,
Where knock is open wide.
CHRISTOPHER SMART, "A SONG TO DAVID"

Home-equity loans are a hybrid. They are among the most popular sources of capital for small businesses but are essentially a secured personal loan. Home-equity loans are so widespread for the following reasons:

- *They allow homeowners to put their home equity to work.* Many people have considerable equity tied up in their house, especially if they have been paying off a mortgage for many years.
- *They are flexible.* There are no restrictions on them beyond the total amount and the repayment terms attached.
- *They are inexpensive*, especially compared with taking a second mortgage or refinancing. Terms are competitive so you can and should shop around.
- *They are easy to come by.* Banks offer them. Near-banks offer them. Finance companies offer them.

But there are dangers attached.

- *For most people, their home is their biggest asset.* Losing it would be devastating, especially for the older borrower.
- *Some harsh terms can be contained in the fine print.* While banks are required to clearly state rates and terms, some finance companies are less than forthcoming—and the penalty clauses can be draconian.
- *Some people want to keep their homes as the equity source of last resort.* We can't recom-

mend that—if things are that bad and you haven't popped your house up the spout, don't do so now!

Every path hath a puddle.
GEORGE HERBERT

Bankers have no desire to own secondhand equipment, or take over your house and chattel. But they know from eons of experience that if you are committed to the venture, and have invested your own assets in it, that you are more likely to work through tough times and thus repay their investment in you than otherwise would be the case.

The role of collateral is to tie you to the deal. Nothing more. If you are unwilling to invest in your venture, why should a bank invest its resources?

For most going businesses, accounts receivable represent a financing opportunity that shouldn't be overlooked. Quality accounts receivable (meaning current, from creditworthy customers) are a prime source of security for short-term bank loans. Banks will lend up to 80 percent on receivables, a much higher figure than they will lend against inventory.

If the receivables are not prime, you may be able to find an asset-based lender or factor who will lend against them, though the terms will be less favorable and the cost higher.

These loans will be either *with recourse* (you have to buy back the uncollectable receivables) or *without recourse* (you sell the receivables outright and have no further interest in them). There are arguments for

Back in 1987, when Michael Troy founded his Petaluma, California, software company, KnowledgePoint, he figured he'd need about $250,000 in start-up capital. "We didn't pay salaries for about a year, and that saved us $80,000. I contributed $24,000, borrowed $20,000 from credit cards, and took out a $50,000 home-equity loan." (*Inc.*, "Anatomy of a Financing: The Benefits of Convertible Debt," February 1995)

When Buddy Pope needed working capital to grow his young company, Recon Services, Inc., his banker suggested he sell some of his invoices to Dallas-based American Receivable Corporation to quickly get cash. That was in 1979. Today Pope still sells his accounts receivable each week, even though his business, which reconditions steel for oil and chemical companies, has more than tripled in size. "Factoring keeps my cash flowing," Pope says. "Big customers pay in 45 to 60 days. By factoring, I get cash every week without loans or lines of credit." (*Business Start-ups Online*, "How to Factor," November 1998)

both—with recourse, you will usually get more money from the lender but have to share the risk, whereas without recourse you will get less money but also be completely shed of the receivables.

There is a very wide difference between getting tenants and getting rent.
GEORGE WASHINGTON

How do you find a good banker? Ask around. Ask other business owners, ask your accountant or lawyer or other advisors, and ask your friends. Think of it as shopping for a partner. What would you do to find a person who can help make your business more successful? A good banker is a terrific asset—so shop around to find a banker you can work with. The role of your banker is to help you make your business successful. A good banker will sometimes do things that you don't agree with, such as turn down a loan request or try to get you to maintain a cautious debt-to-worth ratio. But keep in mind when applying for a bank loan, that bankers dislike risk.

Bankers seek return of principal first, then timely interest payments. Their margins are usually small, in the 1 to 2 percent range, so a loss is difficult to recoup.

Bankers are risk-averse by training and temperament. They can't take the kinds of risks a venture capitalist or private investor might; that isn't their job. They tend to shun start-ups. They hate surprises. This leads to misunderstandings between small business owners and bankers. The relationship between you and your bankers should be businesslike. It certainly should not be hostile or antagonistic or demeaning, yet often it is perceived that way. Cultivate your bankers for their advice and support, have more than one bank, and be prepared to ask why a credit is denied.

Only a life lived for others is a life worthwhile.
ALBERT EINSTEIN

So how do you begin the process of asking a bank to loan your business money? First, you dress appropriately. This may seem like silly advice, but appearances do count. You don't have to don spats and cravat to visit your banker, but do make sure that you are clean, well groomed, and neatly dressed when you apply for a loan. If you are going to make a presentation to a private investor (an angel, for example) make sure to present a businesslike appearance.

Next, fill out your loan application fully and accurately. Loan applications are legal documents—falsifying information on them is a felony under certain circumstances. More important, willfully concealing information can come back to bite you.

Your completed loan application provides the lender with information to make the right credit decision for you. If the information is false, the credit decision may be seriously flawed; while you may get the loan, if the deception is later discovered, your loan will be called and your credit shot.

Do banks and other lenders check the information on your application? You bet they do. It has become increasingly easy to run routine checks via

When Andi and her business partner began to plan their renovation of an old mill, they shopped their business plan around to several bankers before they found someone willing to work with them at their local bank. Not only was he helpful in providing the loan they needed for the restoration—he was also able to refer them to engineers, an accountant, and other professionals whose services were needed for the project.

the Internet concerning employment and credit histories. If there is the least whiff of something wrong, the checks will be more rigorous. Did you really get that MBA from Stanford? Were you really a summer intern at Cravath Swain? Were you a top sergeant in the Marines?

The bottom line: Be thorough and be honest.

Another tip from Andy, a former banker, is to keep your personal financial statement and resume current.

Almost all loan applications call for a personal financial statement. Make your life easier by keeping yours up-to-date. Update it at least once a year. Ditto with your resume—many investors want to see where you have been and what you have done.

These two documents should be complete and forthright. Attempts to gloss over that period when you ran off to Mexico for six months or the embarrassment of being fired (or whatever—we all have skeletons) have a way of coming out at the worst possible time. Think of the "youthful indiscretion" defense beloved of politicians. Yes, I did that. I learned from it and moved on. Here is what I did to rectify it.

And what if you have a bankruptcy in your past? You aren't the only person to go broke. Three key questions that will be raised are:

1. *What caused the bankruptcy?* One of our small business clients had gone through a messy divorce and was sucked into bankruptcy. While married she had signed on her soon-to-be ex-husband's personal and business loans and tax returns. When they separated, his business went under and his taxes went unpaid.

Naturally enough, the creditors (including the IRS) turned to her to satisfy these obligations. She was left with no assets, no job, and no recourse. Under her lawyer's advice she declared Chapter 13 bankruptcy.

2. *What steps did you take to avoid or mitigate the bankruptcy?* This woman made monthly payments for three years as ordered by the court, faithfully and on time.

3. *What assurances can you give that this won't happen again?* This question came up when she applied for a loan to get her small business underway. Bankers tend to believe that the past repeats itself—a reasonable assumption. She persuaded the banker that her business idea was sound, showed that she had been able to make her court-directed payments as promised, and had even been able to put a little money aside to finance her business.

She got her loan. As her banker told us, her frankness about the bankruptcy, her documentation of her side of the story, and her subsequent behavior made her a good risk—and the monthly payments on her business loan would be less than the payments she had faithfully made to the court.

If your credit history needs a jump-start, consider getting a cosigner. A cosigner is someone who "lends" his or her credit to you so you can satisfy a bank or other lending agency's need to mitigate risk. The cosigner agrees to stand behind the loan. If you fail to repay the loan, your cosigner is obligated to make the payments.

Despite heftier sales and triple-digit growth rates, Amazon.com must content with its excessive debt, negative cash flow, and poor inventory management, according to a Lehman Brothers' analyst. Underlying the debate on Amazon is the fundamental question: Can Amazon deliver profits—and how soon? The timing is crucial, because until now, Amazon hasn't had to generate cash or profits. Its growth, critics content, has been almost entirely funded by investors and the debt market. It must begin to replenish its ash through its operations rather than constantly depleting it. (*Business Week*, "Can Amazon Make It?" July 10, 2000)

Why would anyone want to put his or her assets at risk? It may be simpler to cosign than to tie up assets as collateral. Cosigners usually are recruited from friends and family, people who have a lot of faith in your integrity and ability. Andy cosigned a short-term loan for a pal who needed a temporary boost. Cosigning can be time limited: the agreement was that when the loan was repaid, Andy would be off the hook for further loans.

Note that cosigning is not the same as guaranteeing a loan. See Chapter 7 for a description of the SBA's loan guarantee program.

Another bankerly tip from Andy is to use your credit cards wisely.

Many small business owners use the flood of offers for credit cards they receive to keep their financing level. With the low rates available, this may seem like a reasonable tactic. The problem is that cash advances are inordinately expensive, no matter how low the stated interest rate is. Here's why: A cash advance for $100 costs $2 up front, so you are effectively paying 24 percent if you pay the loan off within 30 days.

On the other hand, credit cards are great for travel and for small purchases, yielding you interest-free loans if you pay the balance in full every month.

Some banks have special small business credit cards that are tied to a line of credit. With these cards, there is no penalty on the cash advance, as the bank is saving transaction costs on the loan. Just be sure to abide by the rules of the card.

*A single conversation across the table with a wise man
is worth a month's study of books.*
CHINESE PROVERB

Not sure of how much you really owe on your cards and for other loans? It's always a good idea to check your credit report.

Always get a copy of your credit report before you apply for another credit card. Why? Because your credit history is what companies use to decide who gets a card and—more important—at what interest rate. Credit card companies often reserve the right to charge you a higher rate or offer you a lower credit line than what they advertise depending on your rating, so it pays to make sure your report is accurate and up-to-date. Credit bureaus like Equifax (800-685-1111) or Experian (formerly TRW, 888-397-3742) can send you a copy of your credit history. Fees for reports vary.

You may be surprised at what you find. While theft of identity is rare (it does happen), human error can create a credit nightmare for even the most prudent and financially responsible person.

He that knows least commonly presumes most.
THOMAS FULLER

Andy once got a call from his banker asking about a transaction that just didn't seem right. They discovered that another David Bangs (legal name) with a different middle initial was having severe financial troubles, including unpaid taxes and late payment on business loans. Unfortunately the other Mr. Bangs's credit report had been commingled with Andy's—due to a simple clerical error. To make matters worse, the other Mr. Bangs had an unlisted phone and his enraged creditors kept calling Andy thinking that they'd tracked down their debtor. With the help of the bank, it took about six months to disentangle the credit reports and allot responsibilities to the right parties.

We also advise you to learn the Four Cs of Credit:

1. *Character*. Personal character is most important since all loans to small businesses are in essence personal loans. The bank's experience with you is critical. The judgment on the character of an individual is based upon past performance. Personal credit histories as well as business credit histories will be reviewed.

2. *Capacity*. This is figured on the amount of debt load that your business can support. The debt/worth ratio is often used to justify a credit decision. A highly leveraged business with a high debt/worth is perceived as less creditworthy than a company with low leverage (low debt/worth). Your plan can make a difference here—suppose it shows that the loan will increase earnings and lead to a swift reduction in the debt/worth ratio. Your chances of a positive answer would increase. Keep in mind that a good banker—and you can't afford a bad banker who loads you up with unnecessary debt—is the ultimate realist. Don't try to snow your banker with numbers.

3. *Conditions*. Economic conditions, both regional and national, have a profound effect on credit decisions. If the bank is persuaded that a depression is coming, it won't extend credit easily.

4. *Collateral*. Bankers traditionally wear both belt and braces. Collateral is a secondary source of loan repayment—they want the loan repaid from operating profits and inventory turn so you become a bigger, better bor-

rower and depositor. But just in case things go sour, a bit of collateral makes your banker sleep better at night.

---

*When you get to the end of your rope,
tie a knot and hang on.*
FRANKLIN D. ROOSEVELT

Two more Cs have been cited:

5. *Credibility.* Do you know your business? Can you be counted on to be levelheaded? How believable (credible) are your plans? Are they a collage of dreams or a carefully reasoned and researched plan with a high chance of success? A business plan helps you answer bankers' questions without hesitation, sending your credibility rating soaring.

6. *Contingency plan.* A contingency plan is a useful financing tool. Bankers like to see that you look ahead. A contingency plan proves forethought. What is a contingency plan? It's a short worst-case business plan that examines the options that would be open to the business and how those options would be treated. Decisions made in panic are poor decisions. A contingency plan avoids panic (both yours and your banker's).

When building-contract problems arose, Charles Engberg's architectural firm, Engberg Anderson, had nothing to recommend itself to its banker except the character of its founder and a couple of big projects down the line. As contract bickering dragged on for months, Engberg had to meet an expanded payroll on unexpanded billings. "We got drained," he says, summing up the inevitable result. But Park Bank in Milwaukee came to the rescue. The lender expanded Engberg's credit, asking only good faith as collateral. "They understood the nature of the business and saw us as a company they were willing to take a risk for." (*Inc.*, "Can Your Bank Do This?" March 1996)

> *The most important thing for a young man is*
> *to establish a credit, a reputation, character.*
> JOHN D. ROCKEFELLER

Don't worry about signing loan agreements. If you are squeamish about signing them, it's a clear signal to your banker that you don't believe in your business, your plans, or yourself. Why would you expect the banker to have more faith in your abilities than you do?

Some common elements in a loan agreement are:

- *Prepayment clauses* that restrict or even penalize early repayment of the loan.
- *"Points"* (a point is 1 percent of the total principal amount) may have to be paid on some long-term loans.
- *Compensating balances* may be required. The amount may be specific or it may just be that you use them as your principal bank of account. Some people complain that this means that they are borrowing their own money, which to some extent is true since small businesses are net depositors of funds.
- *Financial statement reporting* is almost universally called for. You will be asked to submit regular financial statements (balance sheet, income statement, funds flow) on a schedule that reflects the confidence that the bank has in your business. A risky business may find that weekly filings are requested, while a safer

business may only have to file quarterly or semiannually.

- *Covenants and restrictions* can include limits on salaries and officer perquisites (no, you can't use our money to lease a Rolls Royce or Gulf-stream jet!), approval before major changes in running the business, a seat on the board of directors, or anything else the lender deems necessary.

- *Personal guarantees* are almost always required. Personal guarantees support the great majority of small business credits. Some magazine article writers and other "experts" argue that you shouldn't personally guarantee loans to your business, but apparently they have never been in business or been bankers. Refuse to guarantee the loan, and prepare to turn elsewhere for financing (which you won't get). Bankers, being realists, know that if you don't have a personal stake in the credit, it's easy to walk away from it. So they will ask you to sign on all notes both as an officer or owner of the business and as an individual. In the real world, incorporation of a small business affords no protection what-soever to the owners. If the business goes broke, the creditors will successfully go after the assets of the owners.

- *Subordinating debt due to officers and owners* is a frequent request. When you subordinate such debt to the bank's loan, it acts as additional capital and may make the difference between qualifying for the loan or not.

Henry Juszkiewicz, CEO of Nashville-based Gibson Guitar, got a $25 million loan in 1997 from Allied Capital Corporation, a Washington, D.C.–based lender to small and midsize companies. "Allied called virtually everybody I know—dozens of people—and asked very pointed questions about me as well as management," Juszkiewicz says. Allied chairman William Walton says he looks for companies to clear certain financial hurdles, like having $1.40 in earnings for every dollar in fixed costs, but the bottom line is that you have to start with great management. "Over the years," he explains, "we've discovered that a good entrepreneur can often achieve more than what the numbers suggest." (*Business Week Online,* "Inside the Mind of a Small-Biz Lender," March 2, 1998)

The wise men of antiquity, when they wished to make the whole world peaceful and happy, first put their own States into proper order. Before putting their States into proper order, they regulated their own families. Before regulating their families, they regulated themselves. Before regulating themselves, they tried to be sincere in their thoughts. Before being sincere in their thoughts, they tried to see things exactly as they really were.
CONFUCIUS

Ask your banker for advice. "I want to expand. Here's the loan I think I need. What do you think?" This is a lot better than asking for the wrong loan at the wrong time in the wrong way. Your banker wants you to succeed—and knows (if he or she is any good) that there is a high correlation between asking for (and heeding) professional advice and making a small business grow profitably.

When you ask your banker for advice you demonstrate:

* *Your respect for his or her advice.* Getting your banker to work with you is better than working without his or her advice.
* *Your interest in securing the right loan or other financing* for your business as opposed to just getting the darn loan. When your banker suggests a different amount or different kind of financing, ask what the reasoning is. You'll learn—and if you have a cogent reason for a different form of financing you'll secure a good hearing.

7

What Does the SBA Offer?

Uncle Sam can be one heck of a friend to small business owners who don't qualify for loans from traditional sources. Through the U.S. government's Small Business Administration's (SBA) loan guarantee programs, more than $40 billion in loans were extended to 491,000 small businesses in 1998 that otherwise would not have had access to such capital.

But according to a 1999 study by Babson College and the Kauffman Center for Entrepreneurial Leadership, thousands of enterprises in the United States are abandoned or never started because their owners didn't know about billions of dollars available from public institutions. To encourage more entrepreneurial activity, the study suggests, among other things, a clearinghouse to detail government programs.

The SBA was created by Congress in 1953 to help American entrepreneurs start, run, and grow successful small enterprises. Today there are SBA offices in every state, the District of Columbia, the U.S. Virgin Islands, Puerto Rico, and Guam; and the agency works with thousands of lending, educational, and training institutions nationwide. Among the services offered by the SBA are financial assistance through guaranteed loans, counseling services, help in getting government contracts, management assistance through programs like SCORE (Service Corps of Retired Executives), and low-cost publications. The SBA even maintains a franchise registry to help franchisees and prospective franchisees receive expedited loan processing. The SBA pays particular attention to those businesses

Jim Newell, a 50-year-old Midas Muffler franchisee in Washington, got caught in the credit crunch of the early 1990s and was turned down for numerous bank loans. But things changed in 1996. Several banks were eager to loan him money, but he signed on for a five-year, SBA-backed $100,000 loan with Kitsap Bank, five years after the bank denied him a loan of equal size. The interest rate was two points over prime, but Mr. Newell explained that his "goal wasn't to get the best rate. It was to get the money." Mr. Newell returned to the bank for a $330,000 SBA-backed loan in 1998 to open three more stores, and they obliged. His six stores will have 1999 sales of $5 million (10 percent of which is profit), and he is currently seeking a $1 million loan to acquire four more Midas franchises. (*Wall Street Journal*, May 24, 1999, p. R6)

owned by ethnic minorities, women, veterans, and others with special needs and circumstances.

The SBA is a great place to start when researching financing options available through federal and state programs. To find the SBA office nearest you, look in the white pages of your phone book under the general heading "United States Government." Or visit *www.sba.gov* on the Web.

SBA financing programs vary according to a borrower's financial need. SBA-guaranteed loans are made by a private lender and guaranteed up to 80 percent by the SBA, which reduces the lender's risk. This enables the lender to provide financing that's otherwise unavailable on reasonable terms.

The SBA's primary business loan program is the 7(a) Loan Guaranty program. It is generally used for business start-ups and to meet various short- and long-term needs of existing small businesses, such as equipment purchase, working capital, leasehold improvements, and inventory or real estate acquisition.

Generally, the SBA can guarantee up to $750,000 of a private-sector loan. The guaranty rate is 80 percent on loans of $100,000 or less, and 75 percent on loans more than $100,000.

Interest rates for 7(a) loans are negotiated between the applicant and the lender. However, lenders generally may not charge an interest rate on loans that exceed 2.75 percent over the prime lending rate, except for loans less than $50,000. The loan can extend to 10 years for working capital and 25 years for fixed assets. Your local SBA office can provide additional details, as can the SBA Web site at *www.sba.gov/financing*.

You never really lose until you quit trying.
                                    MIKE DITKA

If you're a veteran, a member of a minority, a woman, an exporter, or a business owner in a rural area or in certain specialized industries, the SBA Loan Prequalification Program enables the SBA to prequalify you, within limits, for a 7(a) loan guaranty before you go to the bank. An SBA-designated intermediary can work with you to review and strengthen your loan application, apply to the SBA, and, upon approval of the application, find an interested lender. The application will focus on your character, credit, experience, and reliability rather than your assets.

Boldness has genius, power, and magic in it.
                        JOHANN WOLFGANG VON GOETHE

For loans less than $150,000, check out the SBA's LowDoc loans. Bank-qualified business owners do not have to go through the standard SBA application process (the LowDoc application is only one page!) and are guaranteed a loan decision within 36 hours. Loans are guaranteed at 80 percent up to $100,000 and at 75 percent for loans between $100,000 and $150,000. To learn about lenders in your area, contact your local SBA office or check the agency's Web site at *www.sba.gov.*

The SBA offers guarantees for many other types of loans.

When Marshall Rafal needed growth capital for OLI Systems, his chemical-simulation software company, he first turned to an investment banking house to explore his options for equity financing. But when the fall 1998 stock market turmoil deflated the value of many possible private-equity transactions, Rafal decided it made sense to stick to debt. He pursued an SBA loan application that had been wending its way through the paperwork and approval process for nearly a year. Although he says that the SBA insisted on "all kinds of collateral, the loan gave me the funds we need to push our company to the next level, while also allowing me to keep control of our stock." (*Inc.*, March 1999, p. 47)

CAPlines are for financing the short-term and cyclical working-capital needs of small businesses. Five types of loans are offered: Seasonal, Contract, Builders, Standard Asset-Based, and Small Asset-Based. CAPlines loans are generally advanced against existing or anticipated inventory and/or accounts receivable.

Defense Loan and Technical Assistance (DELTA), a joint effort of the SBA and the Department of Defense, was created for defense-dependent small firms that have been adversely affected by defense cuts. Loan proceeds must be used to retain jobs of defense workers, create new jobs in affected communities, or modernize or expand in order to remain in the national technical and industrial base.

Community Adjustment and Investment Program (CAIP) loans aim to create new, sustainable jobs and preserve existing jobs in businesses at risk as a result of changing trade patterns with Canada and Mexico.

Export Working Capital Program (EWCP) provides short-term loans to small businesses for export-related transactions.

International Trade Loans (ITL) offer short- and long-term financing to small business exporters, as well as to businesses adversely affected by import competition.

Energy and Conservation Loans are for small businesses engaged in engineering, manufacturing, distributing, marketing, and installing or servicing products or services designed to conserve the nation's energy resources.

Pollution Control Loans are for businesses involved in designing, building, installing, or servicing a pollution control facility.

The MicroLoan Program provides short-term loans of up to $25,000 for small-scale financing purposes, such as inventory, supplies, and working capital.

504 Loans provide fixed-asset financing through Certified Development Companies (CDCs). These nonprofit corporations are sponsored by private-sector organizations or by state and local governments to contribute to economic development. The 504 CDC loan program is designed to enable small businesses to create and retain jobs—the rule of thumb is one job for every $35,000 provided by the SBA.

The SBA's New Market Initiative, announced in July 1999 by President Clinton, extends special terms to both lenders and borrowers in low- and moderate-income areas nationwide.

Through the SBA's Qualified Employee Trust Program, financial assistance up to $750,000 is available to Employee Stock Ownership Plans (ESOPs).

All growth is a leap in the dark, a spontaneous unpremeditated act without benefit of experience.
HENRY MILLER

To qualify for SBA loan assistance, a company must be operated for profit, be doing business in the United States or its possessions, and fall within size standards. It cannot be a business involved in the creation or distribution of ideas or opinions, such as newspapers, magazines, and academic schools. It cannot be engaged

John and Karen Atwood, brother-and-sister owners of a Harley-Davidson dealership in Boston, expanded their showroom in 1998. To finance the deal, they secured a $1.4 million loan from Century Bank and a $1 million SBA-backed loan from the Mass Certified Development Corporation, a private financing company in Boston. "We liked what we saw in this company," said Elizabeth Trifone, president of Mass Certified. "It was a well-known product and a family-owned business with a long history. They were going to reactivate an ugly building and create jobs. We felt it was a winner." (*Boston Globe*, July 14, 1999, p. D5)

in speculation or investment in rental real estate. The owner must have a reasonable amount of equity in the business and must have used up other means of financing, including personal assets.

The SBA has other eligibility requirements to qualify small businesses. They currently are:

- Manufacturing: from 500 to 1,500 employees
- Wholesaling: 100 employees for financial programs, 500 employees for procurement-assistance programs
- Services: up to $21.5 million in annual receipts or 1,500 employees, depending on the industry
- Retailing: from $5 million to $21 million in annual receipts
- General construction: from $13.3 million to $17 million in annual receipts

You can get the most up-to-date information on size standards by logging on to the SBA's Web site at *www.sba.gov/size*.

To apply for an SBA loan, a small business owner must do the following:

- Prepare a current business balance sheet listing all assets, liabilities, and net worth. Start-up businesses should prepare an estimated balance sheet including the amount invested by the owner and others.
- Prepare a profit-and-loss statement for the current period and the most recent three fiscal years. Start-up businesses should prepare a

detailed projection of earnings and expenses for at least the first year of operation.

- Prepare a personal financial statement of the owner and each partner owning 20 percent or more of the business.
- List collateral to be offered as security for the loan.
- List any existing liens.
- State the amount of the requested loan and the purposes for which it is intended.
- Present these items to a selected lender. If the loan request is refused, the business owner should contact the local SBA office regarding the guaranteed loan program. If the guaranteed loan is not possible, other loans may be available through the SBA.

Supposing is good, but finding out is better.
MARK TWAIN

The SBA also offers some alternatives to bank financing for small businesses. Its Small Business Investment Company (SBIC) program fills the gap between the availability of venture capital and the needs of new or growing businesses. Licensed and regulated by the SBA, SBICs are privately owned and managed investment firms that make capital available to small businesses through investments or loans. They use their own funds, along with funds obtained at favorable rates with SBA guarantees. SBICs make only long-term loans or equity investments, and work

Joe King's Shoe Shop, based in Concord, New Hampshire, filed for Chapter 11 protection. The company, which operates eight stores, ran into trouble because of a shortage of working capital. Shoe vendors weren't receiving timely payments and were requiring the stores to pay for their merchandise with cash on delivery. In March 1998, the New Hampshire Business Development Corporation, a private company that makes loans guaranteed by the SBA, loaned the shoe company $500,000. As collateral, owners Thomas and Judith King put up their home. Although the company is current on interest payments on that loan, a creditor's agreement with the Bank of New Hampshire forbids the store from making principal payments to the New Hampshire Business Development Corporation. (*Concord Monitor*, July 31, 1999, p. B1)

Small Business Investment Companies (SBICs) have provided venture capital to 78,000 American companies, including Intel and Staples. They also accounted for 53 percent of all institutional venture-capital transactions in the United States in 1999, according to the SBA. (*Entrepreneur*, July 2000, p. 128)

with companies whose net worth is less than $18 million and average after-tax earnings is less than $6 million.

SBICs provide funding to all types of manufacturing and service industries, and most consider a wide variety of investment opportunities. For a complete list of more than 177 active SBICs, contact the National Association of Small Business Investment Companies, 1199 N. Fairfax Street, Suite 200, Alexandria, Virginia 22314, or call (703) 683-1601.

Specialized Small Business Investment Companies (SSBICs) are part of the SBIC program and make smaller investments than regular SBICs, often as loans. They invest solely in small businesses at least 51 percent owned by socially and economically disadvantaged individuals. For information and a directory of active SSBICs, contact the National Association of Investment Companies at (202) 289-4336.

Choose always the way that seems the best,
however rough it may be;
custom will soon render it easy and agreeable.
PYTHAGORAS

Sponsored by the SBA's Office of Advocacy, the Angel Capital Electronic Network (ACE-Net) is a nationwide Internet-based listing service that allows "angel" investors to obtain information on small, growing businesses seeking $250,000 to $5 million in equity financing. Introduced in 1996, ACE-Net is not a matching service, nor does it serve as an investment advisor or broker/dealer. ACE-Net was designed to make small direct public offerings cheaper and easier to pull off by eliminating the need for a broker-dealer and lowering the legal barriers. A listing on ACE-Net satisfies many states' securities regulations. You can access ACE-Net at *www.sba.gov/advo/acenet.html*.

Men would be angels, angels would be gods.
ALEXANDER POPE

Aside from its loan guarantees, the SBA offers an array of other programs to benefit small business owners.

- Guarantees for bid, performance, and payment bonds for eligible small businesses that cannot obtain surety bonds through regular commercial channels.
- Assistance for procurement of federal contracts. The SBA's Procurement Marketing and Access Network (PRO-Net) is an online database of information on thousands of small businesses, which serves as a search engine for contracting officers, a marketing tool for small companies, and a link to procurement opportunities. PRO-net can be accessed directly on the Web at *pro-net.sba.gov*.
- Assistance to socially and economically disadvantaged business owners through the 8(a), or Minority Enterprise Development, Program.
- Business counseling, training, and technical assistance through Small Business Development Centers (SBDCs). Often located on col-

ACE-Net is an example of how the Internet can bring investors to the aid of non-traditional candidates for capital. Dan Mitchell, director of the ACE-Net office at Southern Connecticut State University, shares the details of a courtship begun online. A company marketing a diet program was looking for $2 million in equity financing. A group of five angels responded to the initial online pitch. A deal was struck: the angels will kick in $2 million in four installments of $500,000 each and bring some needed expertise to the diet company's management team. (*Inc.*, September 1999, p. 38)

lege campuses, SBDCs are a cooperative effort among the SBA, the academic community, the private sector, and state and local governments. There are SBDCs in every state, the District of Columbia, Puerto Rico, the U.S. Virgin Islands, and Guam. Ask your local SBA office for the location nearest you.

- Access to state-of-the-art computer hardware and software through Business Information Centers (BICs). BICs can provide help with writing a business plan, evaluating sales and marketing techniques, diversifying product lines, pricing, and exporting.
- Expert advice from volunteers through SCORE (Service Corps of Retired Executives). SCORE volunteers are located at SBA offices, business information centers and small business development centers.
- Assistance for funding long-range recovery for private-sector, nonagricultural disaster victims through the Disaster Assistance Loan Program. Eligibility is based on an individual's financial criteria, and low interest rates are available to applicants without credit available elsewhere. Loans are available for homes, personal property, business property, and economic injury.
- In-depth business training for disabled veterans.
- Special programs for: exporters through U.S. Export Assistance Centers, Native Americans through Tribal Business Information

Centers, and women through Women's Business Centers.

- Promoting research and development through Small Business Innovation Research (SBIR) programs. Many federal agencies have SBIR programs—Departments of Agriculture, Commerce, Defense, Energy, Transportation, the Environmental Protection Agency, NASA, and the National Science Foundation, among others.

- Encouraging small business development with awards of federal contracts to small businesses located in HUBZones (historically underutilized business zones).

The sure way to miss success is to miss the opportunity.
VICTOR CHASLES

Thanks to an SBIR investment through the U.S. Environmental Protection Agency, ENOX Technologies, Inc. in Natick, Massachusetts, has successfully transitioned its ideas into a revenue-generating product. ENOX developed a plasma combustion ignition system that assures ignition stability and complete combustion in lean-burn engines. The patented system significantly lowers combustion temperature, improves engine efficiency, and reduces nitrogen oxide emissions. In addition to enhancing engine performance and extending engine life, the system lowers maintenance costs to a fraction of those required for competing technologies. The best news: the cost of ENOX's system is only $40,000 to $102,000 compared with as much as $750,000 for conventional technology. (www.epa.gov)

8

What Are Other Government Sources of Financing?

When some small business owners hear the word "government," they may think of things they wish they didn't have to deal with, like taxes and regulations. But the federal and state governments aren't always takers; they can be great friends and resources to small business owners. Through loan guarantees, technology transfers, grants, and subsidized insurance, government programs have lots to offer growing businesses—not only financing and other financial services but expertise and connections to prospective customers.

Congress requires that federal agencies set aside 23 percent of their contracts for small businesses. In 1999, some $43 billion of the $186 billion the government spent on goods and services went to entrepreneurs. Yet fewer than 3 percent of U.S. small businesses participate in the government procurement programs, according to SmallBusinessDepot.com, a Web start-up that helps link small companies with federal contracts.

We devoted the previous chapter to the Small Business Administration (SBA), the primary advocate of small business within the federal government. In this chapter, we'll take a look at some other government agencies to see what they have to offer.

In early 1999, Pacific Edge Software landed a $125,000 contract to set up project-management software for the U.S. Department of Housing and Urban Development. Officials liked it so much they asked the Kirkland, Washington, company for a license to use the product at thousands of HUD workstations. The $1 million deal gave the fledgling company more credibility just as it was seeking venture capital and helped it raise $32 million in two rounds of financing. Pacific Edge has grown from two to 100 employees and is trying to market to other government agencies. (*Business Week*, "Uncle Sam Wants YOU!" July 31, 2000)

> *There is good government when those who are near are happy, and when those who are far away desire to come.*
>
> CONFUCIUS

Along with nurturing farmers, promoting development in rural areas, protecting natural resources, and ensuring the quality of our food supply, the U. S. Department of Agriculture (USDA) also administers several financial programs to help businesses grow in rural areas.

- *Business and Industry Direct Loans* are available to businesses and public entities (municipality, county, tribal group, etc.) in rural areas that cannot obtain credit elsewhere. These loans (up to $10 million) can be used for improving, developing, or financing business and industry; creating jobs; and improving the economic and environmental climate in rural communities (including pollution abatement).
- *Business and Industry Guaranteed Loans* guarantee up to 90 percent of a loan (up to $25 million) made by a commercial lender to a rural business or public entity. Loan proceeds may be used for working capital, machinery, equipment, buildings, real estate, and certain types of debt refinancing.
- *The Intermediary Relending Program* finances business facilities and community development projects in rural areas. The Rural Business Cooperative Service makes loans to

intermediaries (private nonprofits, public agencies, Native American groups, or cooperatives) who then relend the funds to recipients so they can establish new businesses, expand existing businesses, create jobs, or run community development projects.

- *Rural Business Enterprise Grants* are made by the Rural Business Cooperative Service to public entities, nonprofits, and tribal groups to finance and facilitate development of small businesses in rural areas.
- *Rural Business Opportunity Grants* provide funds for technical assistance, training, and planning activities that improve economic conditions in rural areas.
- *Rural Economic Development Loans and Grants* from the Rural Business Cooperative Service can be used for community facilities and infrastructure (telephone, electric utilities), and for assistance with rural economic development loans.

For more information on the U.S. Department of Agriculture's programs for rural businesses, see *www.rurdev.usda.gov/rbs/busp.*

I learned more about economics from one South Dakota dust storm than I did in all my years in college.
HUBERT H. HUMPHREY

In the summer of 1999, the USDA announced that it was awarding $77.4 million in loan guarantees to start or expand rural businesses in 13 states, areas where unemployment is high. Among those businesses receiving funding are Tangora Seafoods in Oahu, Hawaii, which will get $2.5 million to establish a sustainable, commercial fishing operation and an export-import distribution business. The project will create 92 jobs in an area that has suffered heavy unemployment when sugar production facilities closed. Cardinal Plaza LLC received $3.5 million to build a Food Lion supermarket and several other shops and restaurants in a predominantly low-income neighborhood in Henderson, North Carolina. As the only supermarket to serve the area, the project will create 45 new jobs. (USDA news release, July 21, 1999)

The U. S. Department of Commerce's Commercial Service provides expert advice, information on markets abroad, international contacts, and advocacy services to U.S. firms. These services are specifically designed to help small and medium-size U.S. businesses start or expand their export efforts.

The USDOC's Commercial Service is also one of the lead agencies providing export services through U.S. Export Assistance Centers (USEAC). USEACs are federal export assistance offices that streamline export marketing and financial assistance by integrating in one location the services of the U.S. Commercial Service, Export-Import Bank, the SBA, and the U.S. Agency for International Development (AID).

There are currently 19 USEACs connecting 100 EACs throughout the United States and its territories. For a state-by-state directory that lists contacts' names, addresses and phone numbers, go to *www.ita.doc.gov/uscs/domfld.html*.

The Export-Import Bank, or Ex-Im Bank, is an independent federal government agency that provides financing to small and large businesses and to prospective exporters who've had difficulty obtaining working-capital loans from commercial lenders. Financial assistance is provided through:

- *Small Business Insurance Program*, which offers open-account payment terms for foreign customers. The program protects exporters against payment default by foreign buyers, either for commercial or political reasons.
- *Medium-Term Export Credit Insurance* allows exporters to offer credit terms ranging from

one to seven years, with the commercial and political risks of default covered 100 percent by Ex-Im Bank.

- *Working Capital Guarantee Program* enables commercial lenders to make short-term working capital loans to U.S. exporters for various export-related activities by substantially reducing the risks associated with these loans. These guarantees may be provided for a single loan or a revolving line of credit. Exporters may use the program to purchase raw materials and finished goods for export; to pay for materials, labor, and overhead; to produce goods for export; and to cover stand-by letters of credit and bid and performance bonds.

- *Direct loans and guarantees of commercial financing* help foreign buyers of U.S. capital goods and related services. Both loans and guarantees cover up to 85 percent of the U.S. export value, with repayment terms of two years or more. Ex-Im Bank's fixed-rate direct loans are offered at the lowest interest rate permitted for the market and the term.

- *A special financing program* is available to exporters of environmental products and services.

For more information, visit the Ex-Im Bank's Web site at *www.exim.gov* or call (800) 565-3946.

Pura, Inc. of Valencia, California, used Ex-Im Bank's Short-Term Environmental Export Insurance Policy to significantly expand its export sales. Pura is a manufacturer of ultraviolet water purification equipment and generates three-quarters of its business through export sales with customers in Mexico, Argentina, Indonesia, Turkey, and Italy. According to Pura vice president Ellis Anderson, "Ex-Im Bank's Export Credit Insurance has enabled us to extend the credit terms that our customers needed, resulting in a 300 percent sales increase with our existing customers and winning new ones." *(www.exim.gov)*

OPIC is backing MCT Investors, L.P., a small business based in Alexandria, Virginia, with nearly $16 million in political risk insurance for two telecommunications joint ventures in Russia. MCT has established 900 GSM cellular telephone networks in Yekaterinburg and Siberia. Backed with $33 million in OPIC political risk insurance, the company has established telecommunications projects in Tashkent and Samarkand. "The former USSR provides substantial opportunities for U.S. small businesses," says Richard Seney, CEO of MCT. "But the region has its risks. Political instability, expropriation, and currency conversion are issues we can't influence, and the role of OPIC is essential to our business. Without it, necessary financing would not be available and we would not be involved." *(www.opic.gov)*

The only way to keep score in business is
to add up how much money you make.
HARRY B. HELMSLEY

The Overseas Private Investment Corporation (OPIC) provides the following services to new and expanding businesses in 140 developing countries around the world:

- Insurance against a broad range of political risks for investments overseas
- Loans and loan guarantees for businesses abroad
- Private investment funds to provide equity to businesses overseas
- Advocating the interests of the American business community overseas

For more information, visit OPIC's Web site at *www.opic.gov* or call its Investment Development Department at (202) 336-8621.

The world is an oyster
but you don't crack it open on a mattress.
ARTHUR MILLER

The Department of Energy's Office of Industrial Technologies (OIT) supports the development of key energy-efficient technologies that have applications across a broad range of industries. Both technical assistance and financial assistance are available.

OIT's National Industrial Competitiveness through Energy, Environment, and Economics (NICE3) grant program provides funding to state and industry partnerships (small and large businesses) for projects that develop and demonstrate advances in energy efficiency technologies. These partnerships are eligible to receive a one-time grant of up to $525,000. Applicants should submit proposals through their state energy, pollution prevention, or business development office. Or, for more information, they can call (800) DOE-EREC or visit *www.oit.doe.gov/nice3/*.

Results!
Why, man, I have gotten a lot of results.
I know several thousand things that won't work.
THOMAS A. EDISON

The National Institute of Standards and Technology's Advanced Technology Program (ATP) provides funds on a competitive basis to for-profit businesses of all sizes. The purpose of the program is to promote research into innovative technologies with strong commercial potential but some development risk. The research is directed to technologies that can form the basis for new and improved products, manufacturing processes, and services.

Since 1990, more than half of ATP's awards have gone to individual small businesses or to joint ventures led by small businesses.

ATP projects typically run from two to five years. They're expected to make significant contributions to scientific and technical knowledge, and

Beta Control Systems in Beaverton, Oregon, developed a hydrochloric acid recovery system that met the needs of small and medium-sized manufacturing plants. The key to Beta's system was that all the parts of the potential waste were recovered: the HCl acid was recuperated, the water was reused, and the concentrated iron chloride was sold at a profit. And instead of spending $14 per ton to clean their products, small manufacturers have slashed that cost to $3.40 a ton. But prior to Beta's efforts, the only HCl acid recovery technology that existed was for large-scale steel manufacturers. In 1993 NICE3 awarded Beta and the Oregon Department of Energy a $97,000 cost-shared grant to help the company market its system. "It also allowed us to present our system to an international forum," said Bryan Cullivan, Beta president and founder.
(www.oit.doe.gov/nice3)

yield substantial benefits to the economy beyond those accruing directly to the grantee. Among the 17 focused programs that ATP holds special competitions in are the following:

- Adaptive learning systems
- Digital data storage
- Information infrastructure for health care
- Tissue engineering
- Tools for DNA diagnostics
- Materials processing for heavy manufacturing
- Motor vehicle manufacturing technology
- Vapor compression refrigeration technology

For more information and to receive a proposal preparation kit, call (800) ATP-FUND, (800) 287-3863, or visit *www.atp.nist.gov*.

If I have been able to see farther than others,
it was because I stood on the shoulders of giants.
                                    SIR ISAAC NEWTON

The Minority Business Development Agency provides business development services for minority-owned firms. Their nationwide network of Minority Business Development Centers for new and growing businesses helps minority business owners find financing and provides them with assistance for bonding, bidding, procurement, international trade, franchising, acquisitions, and joint ventures. For a complete listing of these centers, visit *www.mbda.gov* or write the U.S. Department of Commerce, Minority

Business Development Agency, 14th and Constitution Ave. N.W., Room 5084, Washington, D.C. 20230.

For many veterans with severe service-related disabilities, self-employment is their only option for rehabilitation. The Veterans Administration offers help in the form of training, supplies, essential equipment, and technical assistance.

The federal Plan for Achieving Self-Support (PASS) program can help people set aside funds to start a business without jeopardizing their Social Security Income benefits and Medicare coverage. To qualify for the PASS program, applicants must have completed a business plan that demonstrates how the business will lead to self-sufficiency. Applications are available at local Social Security Administration offices.

State offices of vocational rehabilitation are another resource for helping entrepreneurs with disabilities. Some offer financial assistance to help clients get their businesses off the ground. Others, like the RISE (Reach Independence through Self-Employment) program in Maryland, work with SBDCs (Small Business Development Centers), chambers of commerce, and colleges to provide funding, training, and market analysis to clients who own at least 51 percent of the business and are able to operate it.

Each state has an office or agency that acts as a clearinghouse of information on financial programs and services for small businesses. In addition to information on state programs, these offices also provide information on federal and local programs for small businesses. Among the kinds of financial assistance available on the state level are guaranteed, direct, and

Schafer Corporation, a Chelmsford, Massachusetts, firm that provides technical and professional services and consulting to industry and the government, has received a three-year, $2.3 million award from the National Institutes of Health to support ongoing research, development, and commercialization of Schafer's neurostimulator device, the Optically Switched Microelectrode Array (OSMA). OSMA is a semiconductor device that allows researchers to record from or stimulate tens of thousands of neurons simultaneously to better understand neurological disorders and how the brain processes information. Schafer hopes to have a commercially available product within the next couple of years. (*Boston Globe*, August 11, 1999, p. D4)

The New York State Banking Department offers the Renaissance Small Business Loan Fund through its Manhattan Neighborhood Renaissance Local Development Corporation (LDC). The program provides women and minority small business start-up loans ranging from $500 to $50,000 for working capital and equipment and plant needs. Businesses that are located below 14th Street in Manhattan are eligible. For more information, call the Manhattan Neighborhood Renaissance LDC at (212) 979-8988. They're located at 180 Eldridge Street, New York, New York 10003.

revolving loans; grants; revenue bonds; information on venture capital sources; and tax incentives.

The names of these offices vary from state to state—the Alaska Department of Commerce and Economic Development, Colorado's Office of Business Development, Hawaii's Business Action Center, New Hampshire's Business Finance Authority, and the West Virginia Development Office. About the only thing these offices have in common is that they're all located in their state's capital. But additional offices may be located in other cities in bigger states, for example, New York (see sidebar). For a state-by-state listing of state agencies with programs for small businesses, see Appendix Two.

Your best bet as you begin your search for state government money is to check with your local commercial financial institutions first. In addition to having special programs for lending money to small businesses, many of them work with federal or state offices to provide capital through loan guarantees. Some rural areas have Certified Development Companies (CDCs), nonprofit corporations set up to stimulate the economic development of its community or region. For a state-by-state listing of CDCs, go to *www.sba.gov/gopher/Local-Information/ Certified-Development-Companies/.*

It marks a big step in a man's development when he comes to realize that other men can be called in to help him do a better job than he can do alone.
ANDREW CARNEGIE

9 | Do Any Nongovernment Organizations Offer Small Business Financing?

There are literally thousands of nongovernment organizations (typically nonprofits) throughout the country with loan programs targeted to very small business, or microbusiness, owners. These programs range from providing "microloans" of $500 to $25,000, and sometimes higher, to facilitating $100,000 lines of credit. Unfortunately, most of these programs are very local in nature and there's no real consistency on a state-by-state basis. Although scattered throughout the country, a majority of the programs are located in the Northeast and West, according to Bill Edwards, the executive director of the Association for Enterprise Opportunity (AEO), a growing trade group for more than 500 microenterprise development organizations headquartered in Chicago.

By definition, microbusinesses range in size from sole proprietorships to those businesses employing up to five people. Here in New Hampshire, where we live, microenterprises comprise the largest number of businesses in the state, according to the Business and Industry Association of

Mark Scheinberg has been running a for-profit trade school since 1981, originally known as Data Institute Business School, in East Hartford, Connecticut. In the late 1980s, when a local nonprofit offered a $50,000 grant to teach women "nontraditional" occupations, he had an electronics program going within weeks. Now, his school is accredited by the state of Connecticut and is known as Goodwin College; it provides two-year degrees in office technology, computer electronics, and medical assisting. (*Wall Street Journal*, August 24, 1999, p. B2)

New Hampshire. However, microenterprises generally face bigger challenges because they have less access to capital, training, and markets than larger businesses do.

Bill Edwards tells us that his organization is trying to improve coverage of local programs by getting involved with new groups around the country. He urges business owners who want to be directed to the microlending program closest to them to send an e-mail request to the Association for Enterprise Opportunity (AEO) at *aeo@assoceo.org*.

No one ever got very far by working a 40-hour week. Most of the notable people I know are trying to manage a 40-hour day.
CHANNING POLLOCK

Another resource for finding microcredit lending programs in your state is the Grameen Foundation Web site at *www.grameenfoundation.org/replications/domestic4000.html*. The Grameen Foundation-USA is a nonprofit created to collaborate with public and private institutions to achieve the long-term goal of eliminating poverty in the United States and throughout the world.

Grameen began the microcredit movement in 1976, when an economics professor gave tiny loans to 42 workers under a system that would later become Grameen Bank in Bangladesh. Since then, more than $1 billion has been loaned to millions of borrowers in more than 65 poverty-focused microcredit programs in 44 countries. Training and other support are also provided.

A gold mine of information on microenterprise has been collected by the Aspen Institute, an educational institution based in Washington, D.C. Two of Aspen's projects have shed lots of light on microenterprise and self-employment: the Self-Employment Learning Project (SELP) and the grant-making Fund for Innovation, Effectiveness, Learning and Dissemination (FIELD).

FIELD's Web site, *www.fieldus.org*, provides a lot of information on grants, microenterprise development, and leading practitioner organizations in the United States. One of FIELD's first grant-making projects was selecting five organizations to receive grants that would help them experiment with new ideas and approaches for providing capital to low-income entrepreneurs. We'll tell you a bit about these five organizations, so you can get an idea of the variety of programs available to microentrepreneurs.

The first recipient was Accion U.S. Network, based in Somerville, Massachusetts. The organization is part of Accion International, a private, nonprofit group dedicated to reducing poverty by providing loans and other financial services to low-income people starting their own businesses in 14 Latin American countries and 10 U.S. cities.

Accion's programs target Latino clients in New York, Chicago, San Diego, Albuquerque, El Paso, San Antonio, Houston, and Texas's Rio Grande Valley. As of 1999, the Accion U.S. Network had provided more than $17.8 million in loans to more than 3,000 small business owners. Accion associates serve as

Ivette Alvarez and her husband, Eddy, used Accion's help to expand J&L Statuary, which produces some 2,500 plaster statues and other decorative objects each month. Business is now so good that they have six employees. But in the early 1990s they were working out of the basement of their apartment building and had to turn to local moneylenders to avert a cash-flow crunch. They borrowed $1,000 with a weekly interest of 5 percent, which quickly began to cripple their business. In 1994 they got a three-month loan for $1,000 from Accion with a 16 percent annual interest rate. Since then they have repaid other loans, including one for $24,000, which was used to pay off the last debt to the local moneylenders, move the business to larger quarters, and buy new equipment. (Ford Foundation Report, Spring/Summer 1998)

Little Blessings Child Care is one of nine child-care providers in Maine that received financing from Coastal Enterprises, Inc. (CEI) in 1998. Its new or expanding facilities will result in an additional 307 openings for children in seven communities and will create 40 new jobs in child care. (CEI 1998 Annual Report)

intermediaries, negotiating for loans and lines of credit with traditional banks and then "retailing" those funds in amounts ranging from $500 to $25,000 to microentrepreneurs. They also offer their clients business development services—accounting, legal, marketing, and business planning—through a network of community organizations. For more information on the Accion U.S. Network, visit their Web site at *www.accion.org.*

To open a shop is easy, to keep it open is an art.
CONFUCIUS

A second organization to receive an Aspen grant was Coastal Enterprises, Inc. (CEI) in Wiscasset, Maine. CEI is a private, nonprofit community development corporation engaged in a range of housing, commercial, and economic development activities. CEI began microlending in 1980 to small farms and natural resource–based businesses. Since then, it has provided more than $7 million in financing to more than 500 businesses and technical assistance to 8,000 entrepreneurs. In 1998, almost half of CEI's clients were women.

CEI offers a range of financing, from microloans of $500 to larger loans of $300,000 and up. These loans are made to women, low-income and minority entrepreneurs, child-care businesses, small manufacturers, and young businesses unable to obtain credit through conventional sources. CEI also makes equity investments in growing Maine companies that can generate above-average returns while creating quality jobs and meeting other social goals. CEI requires that each loan or investment must create and target jobs to low-income people or provide an opportunity for a low-income entrepreneur. For more information, write to CEI at P.O. Box 268, 36 Water Street, Wiscasset, Maine 04578 or call (207) 882-7552. You may send them e-mail at *cei@ceimaine.org* or visit their Web site at *www.ceimaine.org*.

The reason a lot of people do not recognize an opportunity when they meet it is that it usually goes around wearing overalls and looking like hard work.
THE CHRISTIAN SCIENCE MONITOR

Community Ventures Corporation (CVC) in Lexington, Kentucky, is a nonprofit community economic development corporation that has served Kentucky's Bluegrass Region since 1982. It has loaned more than $1.1 million to 231 entrepreneurs; in 1998 nearly two-thirds of its clients were women and 71 percent were minorities. In addition to business loans and technical assistance, CVC is also providing a consumer loan product for business loan customers who experience personal financial needs that draw cash out of the business. CVC is located at 1450 North Broadway, Lexington, Kentucky 40505, and may be reached by calling (606) 231-0054.

The fourth organization to receive Aspen Institute funding is the New Hampshire Community Loan Fund, a Community Development Financial Institution (CDFI) that provides loans to support affordable housing, as well as self-help and economic develop-

Sandy Webber, owner of Andy's Chest, a gift shop in Amherst, New Hampshire, said her loan from the Community Loan Fund helped "increase our Christmas inventory. Every penny we make goes back into the business. This has increased both our clientele and the value of our other merchandise." (New Hampshire Community Loan Fund Fifteenth Anniversary Annual Report)

Darlene Sealls's video-editing company needed $50,000 in start-up capital to purchase a high-tech computer system. But local bankers refused to provide a credit line because she had no corporate credit history. She couldn't use credit cards to finance the expensive equipment purchase, and leasing companies also rejected her because she was a start-up. With the help of the Chicago Women's Business Development Center, Sealls applied for a microloan from Evanston Business Investment Corporation, a nonprofit economic-development group. Although Sealls was only able to borrow $10,000, she tapped her personal savings and started to build a corporate banking history. (*Inc.*, "Banking: The Microloan Alternative," February 1996)

ment. Loans are made in amounts ranging from $500 to $5,000—amounts that may not be available through banks, especially if the business owner hasn't established credit. The Fund made its first microloan in 1987 and is now expanding its peer-lending program statewide. It also offers lines of credit to municipalities and other local development organizations that have business counseling and/or underwriting capacity, but lack flexible capital to make microloans. The Fund is located at 7 Wall Street, Concord, New Hampshire 03301 and may be reached by calling (603) 224-6669.

Every man is the painter and the sculptor of his own life.
ST. JOHN CHRYSOSTOM

West Central Wisconsin Community Action Agency, Inc. (West CAP), serving low-income residents in seven rural counties, began its microenterprise program in 1991 by providing technical assistance and training, and added a loan fund in 1992. Loans range in size from $150 to $15,000.

Aspen's grant to West CAP will help them provide equity to businesses facing cash-flow issues in their early years, when owners of tiny businesses often face the trade-off of taking a salary or reinvesting in their business. West CAP's Business Investment Trust will hold in escrow 40 percent of each loan payment; after 12 consecutive months of on-time repayment, the client can access the funds to invest in inventory, equipment, or working capital. West CAP is located at 119 West 6th Avenue, Menomonie, Wisconsin 54751 and may be reached by calling (715) 235-8525.

As funding shifts more from Washington, D.C., to the states, state governments have become more important financial resources for community economic development. More than 3,600 community development corporations (CDCs) across the country create jobs through business and commercial development activities, as well as produce affordable housing.

For information about CDCs in your state, visit the National Congress for Community Economic Development's (NCCED) Web site at *www.ncced.org* and click on "State Associations." There you can read about the Western Massachusetts Enterprise fund for microbusiness lending and technical assistance; two Portland, Oregon, CDCs that have a microlending program for child-care providers; Wisconsin's business incubator and business assistance program; and lots of other programs in other states.

Genius is one percent inspiration,
ninety-nine percent perspiration.
Thomas Alva Edison

Some CDCs have microloan funds specifically targeted to business owners with disabilities, according to Rose Anne Herzog in her book *Unlikely Entrepreneurs: A Business Start-Up Guide for People with Disabilities and Chronic Health Conditions* (the book is available for $21.95 from North Peak Publishing, (800) 733-9712). The New Jersey Community Loan Fund offers funds for start-up and expansion to entrepreneurs with disabilities, as do funds in Maine, Michigan, and Pennsylvania.

The Lakota Fund, in Kyle, South Dakota, provides loans up to $25,000 to the Lakota people, along with ongoing technical assistance and a seven-week training course. "Our main function is to lend money, but our mission is to develop people," says executive director Elsie Meeks. "We're starting businesses, but we're also building a nation." The Lakota Fund also operates an arts-and-crafts marketing program and serves as a wholesale distributor of artisans' works, which are available on the Fund's Web site at www.lakotafund.org. (*Fast Company*, December 1999, p. 111)

To expand her business to meet the demand for her floral arrangements, Rita Rondina secured a loan from North Carolina's Center for Community Self-Help after commercial banks turned her down—even though her sales had gone from zero to $2 million a year, with every operation crammed into a 6,000-square-foot space. Her loan helped her business grow to support 52 full-time employees and 16 part-timers, with sales of $7 million from a 26,000-square-foot leased building. Her employees, most of them minority women, receive health insurance, paid vacations, YMCA memberships, and other benefits. (*The Ford Foundation Report,* Summer/Fall 1997)

Socially and economically disadvantaged entrepreneurs thinking about starting a businesses may be interested in the Trickle Up Program, based in New York City. Trickle Up works with local community development organizations and is aimed at the underemployed, the working poor, and those transitioning off welfare. In addition to New York, the program serves Connecticut, Pennsylvania, California, Iowa, Vermont, and Maine, as well as 40 other countries around the world.

Trickle Up's goal is to alleviate poverty by helping people start microenterprises. It provides basic business training and offers a $700 conditional grant for working capital. Trickle Up is viewed as a "pre-loan" program, since many of its participants graduate to microloan programs.

For more information, visit Trickle Up's Web site at *www.trickleup.org* or contact the program at 54 Riverside Drive, New York, New York 10024, (212) 362-7958.

'Tis looking downward makes one dizzy.
ROBERT BROWNING

A final program worth mentioning is the Center for Community Self-Help program in Durham, North Carolina. The center is supported by a variety of funders, including the Ford Foundation, and its strategy is based on the belief that helping people accumulate assets like a home or a business is a key steppingstone out of poverty, giving them a toehold on economic security. Today Self-Help manages total assets of $130 million and has become a major force for economic development in North Carolina and one of the nation's leading community development financial institutions.

The gods help them that help themselves.
AESOP

How do you find out what nongovernment organizations offer financial help to small businesses in your area? As we said in the beginning of this chapter, you can send an e-mail request to the Association for Enterprise Opportunity (AEO) at *aeo@assoceo.org* and inquire as to which microenterprise programs serve business owners in your area. You should also ask your banker and contact your state economic development office for leads about local programs. See Appendix Two for a state-by-state listing of state economic development offices.

Acquaintance:
a person whom we know well enough to borrow from,
but not well enough to lend to.
AMBROSE BIERCE

Fleet Boston Financial Corp. has committed $17 million over five years for technical assistance, and it recently joined with an agency in Hartford, Connecticut, to provide $2.5 million for microloans. A few states are getting in on the act, too. Pennsylvania has injected $17.8 million in loan capital and grants for technical assistance into microenterprise agencies. Iowa's Institute for Social and Economic Development offers state-backed loan capital to low-income entrepreneurs. Jason J. Friedman, vice president of Iowa's Institute for Social and Economic Development, says, "Economic development is not just about high tech and large projects. It's also about beauty salons, alteration shops, and auto repair." (*Business Week*, "A Lending Hand," February 22, 2000)

SECTION III:

Making the Most of Your Money

10

Why Is a Well Managed Cash Flow Key to Obtaining Financing?

Survival in the small business world depends upon cash flow. Although big companies can survive protracted periods of negative cash flow, small companies, especially fast-growing small companies, cannot.

If you learn only one financial skill, make it be managing cash flow. Your cash-flow budget combines all the necessary skills: projections, how to tie the marketing elements to the financial resources, establishing quantitative benchmarks and time frames, measuring deviations. A business plan makes the cash-flow projections the basis of useful budgets. This is also the heart of any adequate financing proposal. A financing proposal that is not based on cash-flow analysis won't get much of a hearing from prospective investors.

Positive cash flow equals survival. Positive cash flow buys time, builds assets and profits, and keeps suppliers, bankers, creditors, and investors smiling. Without positive cash flow, survival becomes questionable. Negative or feebly positive cash flow is painful, and unless corrected will either kill a business or damage it so seriously that it never lives up to its potential.

While short periods of negative cash flow occur in almost every business, cash flows have to be positive at least on an annual basis. Some farmers do very well indeed with cash flows that are strongly negative for 11 months of the year. So do some manufacturers, especially those in the garment trade. The key is that they know what their cash flow patterns are—and take steps to finance the negative periods, offsetting that cost against the occasional strong positive cash influx from operations.

Survival of the fittest.
HERBERT SPENCER, *PRINCIPLES OF BIOLOGY*

Unfortunately, the smaller and more thinly capitalized the company, the less able it is to survive extended negative cash flows. This is one reason so many start-ups fail. The business idea may be terrific, but sales always come much more slowly than expected while cash goes out twice as fast. And the initial investment is rarely enough to tide the business along until cash flow turns and stays positive.

How can a small business attain positive cash flow? Discipline. A cash-flow budget is an unbeatable tool if used carefully. If there is to be just one financial statement you use, make sure it's the cash-flow pro forma. It acts at once as a cash-flow budget and as a benchmark for sales.

Cash-flow budgets have kept many businesses going until their management acquires more financial skills. A cash-flow budget teaches liquidity (cash availability), which is more important to survival than profitability. How can you run an unprofitable business? By maintaining a positive cash flow. While this won't last forever, because ultimately cash flow and profitability are closely related, it can paper over short-term gaps. Companies without cash-flow budgets invariably fail. They become unbankable, a term applied to businesses that have no appeal to ordinary lenders and investors.

While a loss on the profit and loss statement (P&L) can reflect a negative cash flow, it doesn't have to. For example, publishing companies enjoy some accounting foibles such as deferred income (which understates sales by deferring revenues to a later period). The cash may come in in December, but since the revenue is not earned until the following year, the company can show a nice loss for tax purposes while enjoying strongly positive cash flow. When he owned Upstart Publishing Company, Andy spent a lot of time explaining this to his banker. He'd look at Upstart's P&L, gag, and ask if the company was going broke. It wasn't, but the P&L didn't show it.

Emphasize timing. Timing is everything for cash flow—the timing of receipts, the timing of transfer of cash, even the dates bills fall due or discounts can or cannot be taken. While timing is always important in business, it is especially important in managing cash flow. A P&L can stand a bit of looseness—it doesn't matter whether a bill is received January 31 or February 10. That 10 days can make a big difference in cash flow if the bill falls due before you have the cash in hand to pay it.

Cash flows are manageable because you have some discretion over the timing of payments. Loan

One month after its launch, PlanetAll.com's founders Warren Adams and Brian Robertson realized that their company had burned through all its capital and was $150,000 in debt. "I thought we were in good shape because we had hundreds of thousands of dollars in the bank," Adams says. In the rush of raising money and creating software to set up its site, PlanetAll.com had neglected to monitor operating expenses. To resolve their immediate cash-flow crisis, the founders persuaded most employees to accept deferments of salary and bonuses, and then set out to raise a half-million dollars. In 1998, Amazon founder Jeff Bezos put a $100 million acquisition offer on the table, which PlanetAll accepted. (*Success*, April 1999, pp. 28–29)

One way for small businesses to conserve working capital is to finance annual insurance premiums. Rather than pay $2,500 to $100,000 up front for a commercial insurance policy, companies can ask their insurance agents to arrange financing that allows monthly installments. This easy-to-arrange source of funds can be part of the financing mix for every business, from restaurants, to contractors, to high-tech companies. (*Inc.*, June 1999, p. 15)

terms can be rearranged, creditors can be asked for extended terms, unnecessary or optional disbursements can be postponed. Cash inflows can sometimes be accelerated by asking customers for prepayment or offering discounts for prompt payment. (The first place to look for relief in a cash-flow crunch is accounts receivable.)

You can sacrifice profit for accelerated cash flow. Offer your customers discounts or special deals for prepaid orders. Another way is not taking trade discounts yourself. (At terms of 2 percent/10, net 30, this is painful. It's like *not* earning 36 percent on the cost of goods.)

A budget tells us what we can't afford,
but it doesn't keep us from buying it.
WILLIAM FEATHER

When you seek financing to ease a cash-flow problem, know what caused that problem. We compare chronic negative cash flows to injuries or disease. Negative cash flows appear in three forms:

1. *Acute hemorrhage.* This is where an expense skyrockets or a major source of cash fails to come through. This is the least dangerous form of negative cash flow, as its sources and potential dangers are readily identified. The business equivalent of a tourniquet (slash expenses short-term) or a transfusion (more capital or long-term debt) can then be applied. Of course if there is no tourniquet handy, the

business bleeds to death quickly. This is one reason well-managed businesses have reserve financing available to them, as well as a plan to implement it.

2. *The death of a thousand cuts.* Unless management is alert to the need to stem all unnecessary cash outflows, the business can succumb to an accumulation of myriad small errors and problems. There are so many outflowing trickles that ultimately a sense of hopelessness pervades the business ("Negative cash flow again! Why?"). The only cure for this is tight management of the cash flow, which calls for a budget. This is the single most common cash-flow problem, by the way. It's the one that bankers are quick to identify—and since it betokens sloppy management, it will make financing more difficult to secure.

3. *Idiopathic aplastic anemia.* This is usually fatal. The most dangerous cash-flow disease is chronic sluggishness of the cash flow, where cash flow is a little negative most months, occasionally relieved by a spurt of positive cash flow. A business can trudge along for a long time this way, underperforming its potential until it finally becomes totally illiquid. There is no dramatic event to point to, no single identifiable cause. Hint: Working capital shortages show up as chronic negative or barely positive cash flow.

In his first business, *Inc.* columnist Norm Brodsky took all the business he could get, and sales went from zero to $12.8 million in five years. "We had cash-flow problems all the way," he says, "but I didn't focus on them. I was too busy selling." When a cash crunch forced him to go without a salary for four straight weeks, his wife became upset. "I thought business was fabulous," she said. "I thought sales were going through the roof. How can business be so great that you can't bring home any money for four weeks?" (*Inc.*, "Paying for Growth," October 1996)

To finance expansion, Safeway Inc. of Oakland, California, sold its existing store properties to real estate trusts, then leased them back and used the proceeds to build new stores. The maneuver added no debt to Safeway's balance sheet. There would be an additional tax benefit in years when Safeway might find itself paying the alternative minimum tax: Rather than lose the value of the depreciation deduction, it could continue to deduct the full cost of the leases. (*Inc.*, "Shrewd (and Ethical) Tactics in Off-Balance-Sheet Financing," October 1997)

Happiness is a positive cash flow.
AMERICAN PROVERB

Use your revolving line of credit as a cash-flow tool. If your business has seasonal cash-flow problems, or if at certain periods of the sales cycle more cash goes out than comes in, a revolving line of credit can be the answer. The periods of negative cash flow should show up on the pro forma. Discuss this problem with your banker well ahead of time. Approach your banker with a careful cash-flow projection showing the need for a line of credit and the source of repayment.

Term loans are a cash-flow tool. So are leases (see Chapter 12). Financing or leasing equipment makes more sense than laying out a huge blob of cash up front. Equipment (trucks, machines, other depreciable assets that will be consumed or used up over a period of years) should normally be purchased on term loans or leased. If you are short of working capital, either a working capital term loan (to be repaid from operating profits) or new investment will be called for. Sometimes a sale/leaseback of fixed assets makes sense; it can free up some cash and lower monthly payments (at the expense of profits).

Three rules of work:
1. Out of clutter, find simplicity.
2. From discord, find harmony.
3. In the middle of difficulty lies opportunity.
ALBERT EINSTEIN

Short-term loans are cash-flow tools. Short-term loans cover 90 days or less (for most banks), and should be repaid from one inventory turn. These are most often viewed as inventory loans. You need to stock up for the Christmas rush; you have a burst of sales; you retire the debt—all within 90 days or one sales cycle.

New capital, long-term and subordinated debt, and equity are cash-flow tools. Cash flow drives all debt and equity decisions. Not profit. Not sales. Cash flow is king. One of the most common reasons small businesses fail is lack of sufficient capital. New capital, either from equity investment or in the form of long-term subordinated debt (quasi-capital), is an obviously helpful cash-flow tool. New long-term debt helps by providing a quick boost to cash flow, then stretching payments over a long period.

I've never been poor, only broke.
Being poor is a state of mind.
Being broke is only a temporary situation.
MIKE TODD

The cash flow shows capital needs. A rule of thumb: Look for the deepest cumulative negative cash flow on your pro formas. Then double it. This shows how much capital (permanent capital, not debt) is needed in the business. Working capital (current assets less current liabilities) is *not* the same as invested capital, although it reflects the presence or absence of sufficient investment. Determining the right amount of capital for your own business is

To rejuvenate Revlon and raise about $500 million, chairman Ronald Perelman decided to sell the company's salon-products business and a handful of Latin American brands. One of the problems facing the company was the $1.8 billion debt left over from Mr. Perelman's 1985 leveraged buyout of Revlon. Merrill Lynch warned investors that the company "risks a liquidity crunch" until it sells the units that are now on the block. (*Wall Street Journal*, October 4, 1999, p. B6)

another matter. You have to not only cover the deepest negative cash flows but provide a cushion for the unexpected cash-flow problems that always crop up when you least expect them.

I use not only all the brains I have but all I can borrow.
                                        WOODROW WILSON

Don't borrow from Uncle Sam to help your cash flow. One mode of self-destruction practiced by all too many small business owners is forgetting that withholding and other taxes have to be paid promptly. Better look elsewhere to borrow money; failure to pay withholding taxes is illegal, expensive, and dumb.

Don't assume that profits will guarantee that cash flow will remain positive. You can make a profit and run out of cash. Illiquidity—inability to meet current liabilities—is a common problem in growing businesses. Increased sales become increased receivables, which have to be financed. Inventories have to be larger. Personnel have to be added. New, larger facilities are needed. New equipment is needed. All of these are cash drains, so the next step is (frequently) new debt, which in turn causes a more severe cash drain.

Don't get hung up trying to make 100 percent accurate projections. Some banks and other capital sources like to see five-year P&L and cash-flow pro forma projections. We think that's absurd; a one-to-three-year projection is more than enough to make a credit judgment. Once you go beyond 36 months, a projection is guesswork. (Even that lengthy a period is dubious.) A 12-month projection, broken down by months, is a valuable guide to management. That level of detail doesn't help too much beyond the first year.

Use "rolling quarters" to keep your projections up to date. Every three months, when you perform your quarterly review (you do review your operating results and financials at least quarterly, don't you?) roll your projections forward three months. Thus if your projections go from January through December, in March and April you should extend the projections through the following March. This helps you keep the projections more accurate than once-a-year corrections and makes it much easier to keep your bankers and other investors up to date on where your business is headed.

Expenses are easier to predict than revenues. Expense patterns are especially stable from one year to the next. This makes projections somewhat easier— but the assumptions still have to be made explicit. The documenting process helps focus attention on each expense item in turn, which (with luck and attention) can result in better control over expenses.

For a short-term boost to cash flow, cut expenses. In the short run, reducing an expense is a faster way to boost cash than increasing revenue. A dollar saved is 100 percent profit, while a dollar of sales is not.

Are your revenues on an accrual or cash basis? Accrued revenues are entered when the bill is presented; cash receipts are entered when the cash is paid. The timing difference can be important: A major receivable appears as revenue, but if the money isn't paid for six months (say, on a federal contract), the cash-flow impact can be horrendous.

Max Ladjevardi and his wife, Bibi Kasrai, own Soho Inc, which sells ergonomic computer desks to chains like OfficeMax and Wal-Mart. They figured that they'd have to shell out at least $5 million to finance a factory, machinery, and warehousing space, and to train employees. Their solution: to outsource everything. They contract with suppliers all over the country—a wood fabricator in North Carolina, a bracket supplier in Ohio. No money is spent on advertising, since Soho offers promotional discounts to retailers to land premium shelf space. With this setup, Soho gets by with $395,000 in working capital and fixed assets combined. (*Forbes*, August 9, 1999, p. 78)

Although John Brandon's Via Systems Inc. had annual sales approaching $1 million and big-name clients like Fujitsu, Brandon had enormous anxieties about running out of cash and not being able to expand. Like many entrepreneurs, Brandon thought cash-flow analysis belonged in textbooks. Management consultant Paul Parish implemented a cash-flow analysis going out 12 to 18 months, along with three-to-five-year projections. In looking for inefficiencies in how Via Systems handled money, Parish found the company did an excellent job collecting accounts receivable, but that sales costs were high. He also suggested having a bank credit line and projections for what each new product would add to monthly overhead costs. (*Inc.*, "A Confidence Game," December 1989)

Budgeting makes financing less important. Holding the line on fixed expenses, working with a tax advisor to minimize taxes, figuring optimal inventory and purchase schedules, maintaining gross margins, pricing, marketing (especially positioning for developing businesses), and product or service development lead to better cash flow and higher profits, which makes it less necessary to seek outside financing. Increased sales revenue is probably the most important profit factor, but it does not operate in isolation from the rest of the items on the P&L and balance sheet.

Be as realistic as you can with your projections. Both optimism and pessimism are traps. Too much optimism leads to overinvestment, while excessive conservatism (pessimism) pinches the company's prospects.

Net—the biggest word in the language of business.
HERBERT CASSON

11

How Can You Bootstrap Your Financial and Other Resources?

As a small-office/home-office business owner, you're probably an expert bootstrapper without even realizing it. If you started your business on a shoestring, bootstrapping was, and may still be, your MO. But you don't have to be in business in order to bootstrap. If you were a college student living on peanuts (maybe literally) or spent years as a single parent, the techniques we'll talk about in this chapter will strike a familiar chord.

Bootstrapping can be defined as stretching your assets, financial and otherwise, as far as you can. It's being conservative with your cash, assuming more risks for some finite period of time, bartering, thinking "green," and subsidizing your business assets with personal ones. It's the old trade-off of swapping time for money—in this case, spending more time, instead of cash, in order to reach your business's ultimate goal of generating a positive, healthy cash flow.

Bootstrapping is a matter of degree and isn't always appropriate for some businesses, particularly those in the high-tech or manufacturing sectors. Even though bootstrapping is very effective for both retail and service-oriented businesses—especially those that are home-based—rigorous bootstrapping may be appropriate for only a short time. It's always a matter of degree, and you don't want to take bootstrapping so far that you

Greg Easley and Paul Frischer launched Bottle Rocket Inc. in 1996. The New York City company creates online entertainment products for professional sports teams. Launching their company by carefully budgeting and bootstrapping, the partners initially set up shop in Easley's tiny, two-bedroom apartment. For nearly eight months, the partners plowed everything back into the company and built credibility in the marketplace so investors would be enticed by their prototype games. Easley describes the first year as "kind of a test run, allowing us to iron out our kinks and learn how to use the resources we had." (*Entrepreneur*, "Walk This Way," October 1998)

become "penny-wise, pound-foolish." But the principles of bootstrapping are helpful for businesses of all sizes and at every stage of growth, because they remind us that our resources are finite and precious and that we should treat them respectfully.

I would not say millionaires were mean. They simply have a healthy respect for money. I've noticed that people who don't respect money don't have any.

PAUL GETTY

Barter, the world's oldest form of commerce, is especially prevalent among small businesses that are undercapitalized or just starting out. Business owners can barter for just about any type of goods or services with suppliers or providers of professional services. But barter isn't just limited to start-ups or businesses with a tight cash flow. For example, Andi's father sometimes barters his dental services for those of other doctors. Barter is also used in the corporate world—for example, when companies purchase advertising in exchange for inventory or real estate, often together with some cash.

Now barter is making its mark on the high-tech world. Television networks dole out airtime to members of the online community in exchange for equity in Internet companies. For example, Triad Media Ventures, a venture capital fund in Stamford, Connecticut, offered barter financing to secure equity in seven Internet start-ups. Triad pitched its services as a way for companies to outsource their marketing decisions, and used advertising-industry publications to establish the monetary value of various mediums of advertising.

> *Fair exchange is no robbery.*
> OLD ENGLISH PROVERB

"Keep overhead low" is the mantra of bootstrappers everywhere. Why spend extra funds for supplies, services, and space if you don't have to? The whole point of bootstrapping is to conserve your cash to the greatest degree you can without strangling your business, so you can grow off the cash flow you've got and only borrow funds when you really need to.

Train yourself to buy on promotion—when your favorite paper or pens go on sale, buy them then. If you can afford to and have extra storage space, buy in bulk. Oftentimes, you can get the best prices at the so-called big-box stores, like Staples, Target, and Office Max. But not always. Check around, both via telephone and on the Web, before you make your purchases.

Get the most mileage from services you contract out by doing as much of the work you can yourself. Instead of handing your accountant a shoebox-full of receipts, organize your paperwork and do all the tallying yourself. Maybe you don't need to consult your lawyer for every question. Take advantage of the excellent self-help legal books published by Nolo Press (*www.nolo.com*). For straightforward flyers or postcards, do your own desktop work instead of hiring a graphic designer.

Alex Weiss and his partners wanted to create a national chain of supersize, self-service laundries, but they didn't have enough money to pay for either stores or equipment. According to their projections, it would cost about $750,000 to open one laundry. Their solution: Have everyone from their architect to their lawyer work for them in exchange for equity in Clean Rite Centers, their newly formed New York City company. They also persuaded two major equipment manufacturers to not only sell them equipment at reasonable rates but also to lend additional funds, with payment terms linked to cash flow. One of the partners described bartering as "a long process of convincing, arm pulling and wrist twisting." (*Success*, March 1999, p. 16)

Buying cheap is at the core of what makes Britain's Lloyds TSB (not related to the Lloyds of London insurer) one of the most successful of the world's big banks. Lloyd's frugality is off the charts, and it translates into unmatched profitability. When Sir Brian Pitman became CEO in 1992, he immediately disposed of two company Rolls Royces. Branches use second-class stamps to mail letters that aren't urgent. Seminars are ended before dinnertime, so the company doesn't have to foot bills for dinner. Branches have budgets for everything—and stick to them. (*Wall Street Journal*, December 13, 1999, p. A1)

There were times my pants were so thin
that I could sit on a dime
and tell if it were heads or tails.
SPENCER TRACY

Rather than rush to rent an office, work out of your home for as long as possible. If that's not feasible, find the most affordable space you can to rent. Sometimes you may be able to sublet a room from a bigger organization at a reduced rate, or even find someone willing to let you "squat" rent-free in their space for some period of time. If your skills are in demand, you might be able to swap your services for space. One company, called Office2share.com (*www.office2share.com*) links large companies with surplus offices and start-ups who are looking for office space they can move into on favorable terms without being locked into long leases.

The greater the obstacle the more glory in overcoming it.
MOLIÈRE

A corollary to keeping overhead low is maximizing the resources you've got. Instead of getting top-of-the-line equipment and cutting-edge technology, make due with an older vehicle and computer until you're absolutely unable to. And when you must replace something, try to buy used rather than new. Think third-hand, instead of secondhand, if appropriate.

If you need to read books or magazines in order to keep up with your trade or profession, make use of your library. Borrow books whenever you can. Even if your library doesn't have the book you're looking for, they can often find it at another branch and borrow it for you.

To save on subscription fees, share subscriptions to magazines and newspapers with colleagues or friends. By doing this, you're also being friendly to the environment. And speaking of "thinking green," try to use both sides of a sheet of paper, whenever possible.

When you do need to take out a client, economize by taking him or her to breakfast or lunch. The cost of those meals can be easily a third, or less, of what you might spend on dinner at a nice restaurant.

To maintain a cash-flow edge, know which customers pay their bills quickly and which don't, and take care of the good customers first. At the same time, negotiate the longest terms you can with suppliers, somewhere in the 45- to 60-day range. This strategy will help you avoid borrowing to pay bills, even for a very short term.

Economy is the art of making the most of life.
The love of economy is the root of all virtue.
GEORGE BERNARD SHAW

Another cardinal rule of bootstrapping is to lay out as little cash as possible, as often as possible. Take advantage of giveaways whenever you can. Collect pens, pads of paper, calendars—anything you know you'll need. Trade shows are great places to get freebies. When you attend one, make sure to bring something to carry everything in.

When Kim Hastreiter and David Hershkovits launched their hip *Paper* magazine in New York City in 1984, they bootstrapped by printing 16 pages without cutting them. The two owners, along with two friends who were art directors from the *New York Times*, each pitched in $1,000 to print 6,000 copies, and friends who owned SoHo clubs, restaurants, and stores bought ads for $250 apiece. They even had makeshift offices at the *New York Times* on weekends. The two friends paid off the photo developers and typesetters and proofread ads in the cafeteria. (*Entrepreneur*, July 2000, p. 140)

Barbara Cassani, CEO of Go Fly Ltd., a low-fare airline based in London, monitors costs to keep fares low. This lets the airline offer customers a cheaper way to fly, which makes more customers want to fly. Cassani achieves her objectives by not using travel agencies (customers book flights directly by phone or on the Web) and not serving free food or drink (passengers can buy quality refreshments on board for a fair price). The strategy is a success. (*Fast Company*, May 1999, p. 98)

Computer user groups are great resources, too. Not only can you get inexpensive or free shareware, you can also benefit from other members' expertise.

In addition to consulting with an advertising professional, cultivate your own ideas by collecting direct mail samples. Educate yourself by reading or taking courses, so you can make the most use of an advertising professional's time when you need it.

If your business is a retail one, accept merchandise on consignment whenever possible. This way you don't have to pay suppliers until you have cash from the sale in hand. To assuage suppliers, you can offer them a larger percentage of the sale than wholesale. This is how it works in many craft shops and galleries, where artists wholesale for only 50 percent of the sale price, but can receive 60 percent or more when they consign their work.

Don't forget about government resources. The Small Business Administration offers lots of free services that are valuable to businesses of all types (see Chapter 7). There's also the *Small Business Source Book* at your local library. It's a gold mine of information, including detailed business specific data as well as references to books, trade organizations, consultants, trade shows, and more.

Extraordinary how potent cheap music is.
NOËL COWARD

Whenever you do have to buy, spend within your means, particularly during your critical first year in business. Although we've all seen ads and read stories that glorify entrepreneurs who've started wildly successful businesses using credit cards, we don't hear the stories about those who've failed. Not only do credit cards burden debtors with high interest rates, they can also result in poor credit ratings and even personal bankruptcy if the debt cannot be repaid.

By the same token, be very careful about how many of your personal assets you put into your business. You want to make sure that you've still got a comfortable reserve of cash and savings in case the business doesn't succeed. Selling life insurance and dipping into retirement accounts can come back to haunt you if you decide to fold your business.

Avoid borrowing money and grow off the cash flow you've got. Until your business starts generating cash, keep your day job or be able to live on your spouse's salary. And think twice about selling your products on credit until you're able to write off the debt, should you have to.

No other protection is wanting,
provided you are under the guidance of prudence.
                                                JUVENAL

A final rule of bootstrapping is to carefully manage your business's growth. Not only does it make financial sense, it will help you buy time as you learn the ropes of your business, without a lot of unnecessary pressure.

To boost revenue, Frank DeSocio will spend 5 percent of his annual revenue on renovations to his four bowling alleys in and near Wichita, Kansas. That's double the rate of earlier in the 1990s. He's eyeing an elaborate air-filtration system, at a cost of $25,000, that allows smokers and nonsmokers to peacefully coexist. This is seen as crucial for bowling alleys, because some 50 percent of customers can be smokers. Joe Schumacker shelled out $1.6 million to renovate lanes in Boca Raton and says revenue from casual bowling is up 40 percent annually since then. "We're headed for an ambiance that attracts birthday parties, corporate meetings and other special events," Schumacker explains. (*Wall Street Journal*, September 14, 1999; p. B2)

Paul Aldrich began Village Candle in 1992 with $20 borrowed from a friend. After seven years, the Topsham, Maine, business had grown to $30 million in annual revenues. Aldrich's secret? He limited Village Candle's annual growth to 100 percent. "I could have grown the company 200 to 300 percent a year if I had wanted to borrow money, but then you lose quality control. Our philosophy has been to build the business one brick at a time." (*Inc.*, August 1999, p. 50)

Never be quick to add employees. In fact, the slower you add staff the better off you'll be. When you're bursting at the seams and absolutely must hire someone, look for candidates who are inexperienced but ambitious, or maybe retired but energetic. As Malcolm Forbes so aptly said, "Enthusiasm, not expertise, is the requisite." Although you may not be able to offer a big salary, you can provide lots of intangible benefits, such as flextime, independence, growth opportunities, creativity, a nurturing environment, and so on.

Depending on the type of business you have, you might want to think about running it on a part-time basis at first. Many an Internet business has gotten its start in the evenings or on weekends; such a schedule would, of course, be impossible for retail businesses. If you decide to take the evening/weekend route, make sure that your business doesn't compete with that of your employer. Any questions you have should be directed to your attorney.

Genius is eternal patience.
MICHELANGELO

12

What Are the Pros and Cons of Leasing?

When you think of leasing, you probably think of cars, computers, and office space as things you might lease rather than buy. But did you know that furniture, software, and even employees can be leased? For some businesses, leasing makes good financial sense. For others, an outright purchase is a better deal. Do you know what's best for your particular business, and why?

Leasing is advantageous because you don't finance the entire value of your equipment or furniture—you only pay for that portion you use. As a result, you avoid having to make a down payment and your monthly payments are usually lower than those for financing a purchase are. And because lease payments are considered expenses for tax purposes, they don't show up on a balance sheet as debt. But if you decide to purchase the item you've been leasing when the lease ends, you often wind up paying more for whatever you've leased to account for the lessor's overhead and profit.

The bottom line is that you need to know what your resources, costs, and needs are, and evaluate all methods of financing before you commit to leasing or purchasing any big-ticket item. And make sure you have a thorough discussion with your CPA about which makes better sense for your business—leasing or purchasing.

Instead of paying a head-hunting firm $50,000 a month to find new hires (and the hunters were turning up only three workers a month when the company needed five), Revenue Systems Inc. (RSI), an Atlanta software developer, now gives BMWs to all 60 of its full-time employees. All the cars are leased—RSI pays leasing costs, including insurance and taxes, which amount to $30,000 a month. The reason for the company's largesse? "In Atlanta, there are more than 500 software developers," says RSI chief executive Bill Glover, who came up with the idea for the BMW perk. "It's hard for any company to stand out from the crowd." Now that the news is out, RSI is flooded with resumes. It has no more headhunting costs—and lots of happy employees. (*Business Week*, "And We'll Even Throw In. . ." October 5, 1999)

> *The secret of business is knowing something that nobody else knows.*
> ARISTOTLE ONASSIS

To figure out whether you should lease or buy something, you need to take a look at the big picture in your business. What are your goals, your priorities, and the state of your financial health? Are you in an industry that is experiencing a growth spurt? Do you aim to triple your workforce in the next couple of years?

If you answered yes to any of these questions, then leasing might make sense for your business. Generally, it makes sense to lease an asset that will depreciate, or to lease equipment whose technology is rapidly changing. Leasing also makes sense when any of the following apply:

- There's a risk that the equipment will become obsolete before the end of its useful life
- The equipment will only be needed for a short time
- The business needs to preserve its capital
- Interest rates are high
- Tax benefits resulting from equipment ownership cannot be used

One drawback to leasing is what happens at the end of the lease term, when you have to give whatever you leased back to the lessor. What if you still need the equipment you've been leasing for the past three years? Will the lessor sell or re-lease the equipment back to you, or is a suitable replacement available? These questions are well worth a close look before you sign on the dotted line.

*Be not afraid of growing slowly,
be afraid only of standing still.*
CHINESE PROVERB

If your business is seasonal, or you're working on a project basis, renting might make more sense than leasing. Renting works best when your time frame is short, say several months or less. Rental companies will often work with customers to figure out a favorable longer-term rental fee.

*Control circumstances,
and do not allow them to control you.*
THOMAS A. KEMPIS

Leasing also makes more sense in some economic climates rather than in others. For example, because of a fixed payment schedule, leasing is more advantageous during a recession. You can lock in a lease payment based on a fixed, not floating, interest rate, which gives you a handle on expenses. Leasing also gives more short-term flexibility, which is handy during a recession when some businesses have to make cutbacks in staff or expenditures. In addition, you don't want cash tied up in depreciating equipment at a time when working capital might be tight.

A German subsidiary of Star Telecommunications contracted with Deutsche Leasing AG to provide lease financing for equipment purchases in Europe. Those provisions, now at approximately $45 million, will increase as the company's equipment needs expand. The arrangement allows Star to finance existing and newly purchased equipment through a lease-financing format. Cash generated from these arrangements will be used to help fund the growth and operations of the German business. (Press release from Star Communications, October 4, 1999)

In a growing economy, where inflation and unemployment are low and corporate profits are high, purchasing makes more sense. Buying equipment or other assets outright puts a robust cash flow to work and results in certain tax advantages, such as depreciation. Or an asset might appreciate in value, resulting in additional income when it's sold.

Caveat emptor. *(Buyer beware.)*
LATIN PROVERB

Who can finance the equipment you need to lease? One place to start looking for financing is with the vendor or manufacturer. Many companies, like Xerox, Dell, and Gateway, have a variety of short- and long-term options available for leasing equipment.

Another option is a bank. Because banks have lots of capital available to make purchases, they can pass on a lower lease payment to customers with high credit ratings. They can also be more flexible than leasing companies. But one hitch is that banks generally require the lessee to purchase the equipment for a nominal fee or at fair market value when the term of the lease is up. If the lease term is short, a business owner is usually better off going to an independent leasing company.

If you want to lease employees, contact an employee leasing company, also known as a professional employer organization (PEO). PEOs serve as co-employers, taking control of the personnel administration and paperwork that drive small busi-

In 1980 at the age of 21, William Herman was a principal player in his second start-up failure. His medical software company, Dataware Solutions, went after higher-end, bigger-budget customers; Herman wrote software and sold services on a 24/7 basis. The company had more work than it knew what to do with. In order to write software for all the hospitals, Dataware had to own the same hardware they had. The company purchased close to $100,000 in equipment. "The concept of leasing never occurred to us," Herman says. "As a result, we hit a serious cash-flow problem and went bankrupt after 18 months." (*Forbes ASAP*, May 31, 1999, p. 24)

ness owners to distraction. Most PEOs offer a wide range of services and benefits packages, including payroll administration, medical benefits, workers' compensation and unemployment insurance, retirement plans, and compliance assistance with labor laws. The usual charge is 2 to 8 percent of total payroll, over and above the cost of benefits, taxes, and insurance.

Although employee leasing is growing, employers need to choose carefully. Make sure the PEO you're interested in is accredited by your state and by the Institute for the Accreditation of Professional Employer Organizations in Bethesda, Maryland. Get references and check them.

How do you find a leasing company? Ask your banker, business colleagues, your vendor, or the manufacturer of the item you want to lease. Look in the phone book or do a search on the Web. We found a long list of leasing companies from all over the country at *http://smallbusiness.yahoo.com/smallbusiness/finance*. You can also get a referral for a leasing company by contacting the United Association of Equipment Leasing (520 Third Street, #201, Oakland, California 94607, (510) 444-9235, *www.uael.org*).

Most reputable leasing companies will be registered members of the Equipment Leasing Association (*elaonline.com*) as well as regional leasing associations. Another rule of thumb: The more affiliations a company has, the more reputable it is likely to be.

Wherever you find a leasing company, remember to do your homework. Find out how long the companies have been in business and evaluate their financial stability.

Athens Insurance Center in Athens, Georgia, has been leasing its 10 employees since 1996. The biggest benefit is that the agency is free from having to deal with state labor departments, tax filings, employee problems, and other human resource and administrative burdens. "I was so tied up with corporate matters that I couldn't concentrate on writing insurance and managing an agency," owner Martin Van Horn says. "Now I have a person who answers all my personnel and employment practice questions. When an employee goes to the dentist, I have a form for them to fill out that documents everything—a record beyond any we ever kept." (*Rough Notes* magazine, "Employee Leasing: What Are the Opportunities for Agents?" June 1997)

When Bill and Peggy Kensi took over Royal Laundry of Texas Inc. in 1996, they knew that some focused marketing efforts could give a big boost to the company's break-even sales of $500,000. But they needed new equipment—lots of it and fast. Their request for a loan was rejected by several banks and the SBA's approval process was too lengthy for their time frame. Jim Lahti, president of Affiliated Corporate Services, an equipment leasing company, took an interest in the Kensis and over the next two years structured seven leases for Royal Laundry's equipment. As a result of its expanded capacity, Royal Laundry's business boomed. In two years, sales increased more than fivefold, to $2.8 million. (*Entrepreneur*, "Lease Is More," August 1998)

Fortunately for business owners, equipment leasing is very competitive. Prospective lessees with good credit and viable businesses are highly desirable. Businesses who stretch payments to vendors; businesses with a high number of "NSF" notices, lawsuits, judgments, or frequent changes in banking institutions; or businesses whose owners have personal credit problems raise red flags that can cause lease applications to be turned down.

If you don't have time to hunt down a leasing company yourself, you might want to work with a lease broker or lease underwriter. Their fees are paid for by the lessor and amount to approximately 8 percent of the leased equipment's cost.

Another option is to work with an equipment consultant—look for listings in your Yellow Pages. These consultants will configure an entire office and recommend a lessor. Many doctors and other professionals wind up going this route.

There are three kinds of leasing arrangements.

1. *Operating leases* are shorter-term (less than a year) leases for high-tech and other types of equipment that quickly become obsolete.
2. *Finance leases* are longer-term (more than a year) leases that cover the purchase cost of equipment. These leases generally transfer ownership of the item to the lessee at the end of the term and contain a purchase option.
3. *Sales-leaseback* works for business owners who need to preserve capital; they can sell their equipment to a lessor and lease it back.

Generally, insurance and maintenance are the responsibility of the lessee. But sometimes these expenses can be included in the lease agreement and their payments spread out over time. If this is something that you think might work for you, make sure you discuss it with prospective lessors *before* you sign on the dotted line.

Other questions to ask before you sign a lease are:

- Does it call for a fixed purchase option or fair market option, where you can negotiate the current values of equipment or choose not to purchase?
- Does it include renewal terms or a month-to-month lease option?
- Does it include undisclosed fees, like broker fees, commissions, property taxes, sales taxes, maintenance, insurance fees, or others?
- Does it offer you options in case the equipment you're leasing becomes obsolete?

Who will change old lamps for new ones?
"THE HISTORY OF ALADDIN," *ARABIAN NIGHTS*

What happens if you want to get out of your equipment lease? Try to find someone to assume the lease. If you're selling the business, the new owners are your best bet, assuming their credit passes muster. If you're going out of business, try to negotiate an early termination of the lease. If the equipment has

Two years into Andy's four-year lease for a Quadritek phototypesetter at Upstart Publishing Company, Apple introduced its Macintosh computers and laser printers—and the revolution in the publishing industry was off to a running start. But the $9,000-a-year lease gave Upstart only three outs: It could trade up its Quadritek (not an option, as the Mac had become technology *de rigueur* for publishing), make a lump sum payment to buy out the lease, or just continue making payments until the end of the lease's term. Andy's conclusion: Continue making monthly payments. In those inflationary times it was less expensive in the long run to make monthly payments than to fork over a lump sum, because most of the finance charges had been paid during the first year of the lease.

When Andi and her business partner, Janet Taylor, took over publishing an arts-and-entertainment weekly, they decided to lease two Macintosh computers from Apple. Cash flow was extremely tight and bank financing wasn't even an option for anyone in the publishing business. When rumblings of the coming recession were heard the following year, Andi and Janet decided to cease publication of their paper, even though they were stuck with two more years of a three-year lease agreement. But they were fortunate to find another business owner willing and able to assume their lease. They will always be eternally grateful to Chris Beal, then of *The Princeton Review!*

appreciated (not usually the case with computers, but sometimes the case with industrial and commercial machinery), chances are the lessor will be amenable to finding a buyer or new lessee.

However, if you cannot find someone to take over the lease, the leasing company will sell the equipment to the highest bidder and apply the money toward the lease obligation. The remaining balance is called a "deficiency balance," and must be paid by the lessee.

Don't enter lightly into any leasing arrangement. Seriously consider your ability to make payments for the duration of the lease, along with the financial ramifications of long-term debt obligations should you need to get out of your lease.

Before you invest, investigate.
SLOGAN OF THE BETTER BUSINESS BUREAU

SECTION IV:

Growing Your Business

13

What Can You Expect from Outside Investors?

Our friend Liz Lisk, director of MicroCredit New Hampshire, has had extensive experience dealing with small businesses and it shows. She tells us, "Family and friends can be a very informal way of accessing loans and can feel the least intimidating. Bad credit and collection agencies are rarely employed by these lenders, and additionally they tend to be more generous in regard to interest, loan fees, and late payments. The price borrowers pay for this type of credit is sometimes, however, recorded in more than dollars."

While family and friends are a natural source of funds for small businesses, pay attention to the nonmonetary risks involved with this kind of financing. If all goes well and the business prospers, friends and family may want to influence its management decisions, since they "own" a piece of the business. If it doesn't prosper, they may feel they have been taken advantage of and be resentful—an emotional cost that can be hard to measure. Make sure you give careful thought to the pros and cons of borrowing money from your family and friends.

Acquaintances, people you know casually, can be a source of leads as well as an occasional source of funds. As an example, Maureen Reardon, an artist who heard one of Andy's business planning–seminars at the

After David Cohen bounced around various schools, including Manhattan's Fashion Institute of Technology, he joined a women's panty business and launched a line that would eventually become Undergirl. But his boss didn't see a future for the division and closed it after six months. As a result, Cohen said he didn't trust anyone over 30. That was, until he met René Rofé, age 48, whose eponymous line does $70 million a year in sales. A friend of Cohen's father, Rofé thought he spotted a winner in Undergirl and invested $600,000 for half the company. Although Cohen spent part of the funds for a desk shaped like a rear end, his company sold nearly $1 million worth of panties in 1998, almost breaking even. (*Forbes*, August 9, 1999, p. 66)

Women's Business Center in Portsmouth, New Hampshire, approached him to ask about financing her jewelry business. After several meetings he wrote her a modest check and urged her to meet with a local philanthropist who was so taken with her work that he wrote her an immodest check—enough to promote her artwork professionally. While this kind of support rarely happens, it does occur. It takes moxie or chutzpah or both, but if you believe in your work and persist, you may find that your effort is rewarded.

The holy passion of Friendship is of so sweet and enduring a nature that it will last through a whole lifetime, if not asked to lend money.
MARK TWAIN

The rapport that develops over time between a mentor and mentee can lead to financing on a larger scale. Andy helped another entrepreneur secure financing for her children's clothing venture by introducing her to several deep pockets he knew would be impressed with her ability and drive. While her business eventually foundered due to the distractions of a divorce, her investors (who could easily afford the loss) were surprised and moved when she insisted on working out individual payouts with each investor.

Will this entrepreneur be able to raise substantial money for a further venture? Unquestionably. Andy spoke with her banker and her lead equity investors after her decision to repay them. They are actively looking for other ventures where the combination of their cash and her abilities can make something good happen.

A true teacher defends his pupils against his own
personal influence. He inspires self-distrust.
He guides their eyes from himself to the spirit
that quickens him. He will have no disciple.
                                A. BRONSON ALCOTT

There are several other ways investors can invest in small businesses. Private limited partnerships are one possibility. Accredited investors in private limited partnerships must have a net worth of at least $1,000,000 or an annual income of at least $250,000, or put at least $150,000 (which can't exceed 20 percent of his or her net worth) into the partnership. This allows the private limited partnership to raise more capital than would be possible if only 35 less wealthy people invest.

Angels are private investors who plug the capital gap, defined as risk capital investments, between $250,000 and $5,000,000. These sums are notoriously difficult to raise, too small for venture capital firms but too large for most investors. Angels tend to invest locally in businesses that they thoroughly understand.

How do you find them? Network vigorously: Ask your professional acquaintances (bankers, lawyers, and accountants). You can also get in touch with business incubator managers through the National Business Incubation Association (20 East Circle Drive, Suite 190, Athens, Ohio 45701; *www.nbia.org*) or

In 1993 when Iris Shur and Jean Sifleet decided to open a shop selling furniture and home accessories on consignment, they asked experienced business owners to show them the ropes. The rookies paid $1,500 for their day-long lesson and agreed not to set up shop within 50 miles of their Rhode Island mentor's store. After five years, Shur and Sifleet's Acton, Massachusetts, business called Tables to Teapots grew to $600,000 in revenues. And the two have been hired to mentor a few fledgling entrepreneurs themselves. "If we didn't learn from somebody else, it would have taken us a hell of a lot longer to get to where we are now," Shur says. (*Inc.*, "Hands On: Mentors for Hire," December 1998)

Since founding his microwave popcorn company, Kenny Carlson has invested about $30,000 of his own money. But his company really started cooking when Carlson's angels invested a total of about $60,000. One is a personal friend, but the other two had tried Carlson's Cajun Corn and contacted him through his Web site, which is listed on the popcorn bag. Carlson's angels will receive royalties from Kenny's Cajun Corn for the first two years and a slice of the profits for the next two to four years. Carlson hopes to pay back their investment within the first two years. (*Kiplinger's Personal Finance* magazine, September 1999, pp. 125–129)

through your local chamber of commerce, economic-development authority, or area college.

---

*Things don't turn up in this world
until somebody turns them up.*
JAMES A. GARFIELD

ACE-Net, or the Angel Capital Electronic Network sponsored by the Small Business Administration (see Chapter 7 for more information), has a fine list describing angels. This is taken from ACE-Net's excellent Web site at *www.sba.gov/advo/acenet.html.*

- Angels typically invest in ventures involved in markets and technologies with which they are familiar.
- They invest relatively close to home, typically within one day's drive or a flight permitting return that day.
- They are "active" investors, serving on a working board of directors or providing guidance through an informal consulting/ mentoring role.
- As a group, private investors prefer to invest at the seed and start-up stages in the life of the venture.
- They are patient investors. Exit horizons tend to be five to 10 years or more.
- A round of angel financing is typically less than $1 million and, in most cases, less than $500,000.

- Angels tend to co-invest with trusted friends and business associates. The size of one investor's participation in a round of financing is usually in the $25,000 to $100,000 range.
- Angels often take bigger risks or accept lower rewards when they are attracted by the non-financial characteristics of an entrepreneur's proposal. They are, quite literally, "adventure" investors.
- Their investment terms and conditions tend to be more brief and more informal than those of venture capital funds.

---

*Diligence is the mother of good fortune, and idleness,
its opposite, never brought a man
to the goal of any of his best wishes.*
MIGUEL DE CERVANTES

ACE-Net's Web site is a wonderful resource that contains the most up-to-date information on angel investors, including local "angel networks" such as the MIT Technological Capital Network. If you are looking for angel money ($250,000 to $5,000,000), this is where to start. If you are not looking for such a large amount, angel financing is probably not for you.

---

*Who waits on fortune's knock will rarely win;
Who calls on fortune, some day finds her in.*
ARTHUR GUITERMAN

Curtis Giesen, a Harvard MBA, wrote a business plan for MTV's *Loveline* cohost Dr. Drew Pinsky's new Web venture called Drdrew.com. After pitching it 100 times in a year to no avail, Giesen contacted Guy Kawasaki and his band of angel investors at Garage.com. They liked what they saw and immediately listed the business plan in "Heaven," the password-protected section of Garage.com where investors can find start-up companies that match what they're looking for. Soon the online courting culminated in a private-equity deal that raised $1 million in exchange for 20 percent of the company. (*Inc.*, September 1999, pp. 35–36)

Venture capitalists are at the top of the investment food chain. Due to the heavy costs they incur in performing due diligence (a fancy way of saying examining your business proposition from every possible angle, including background checks on the principals), they look for extremely high returns in a short time frame, and the average investment size is now on the order of $7,000,000. Early-stage investments in 1995 showed that 74 seed deals (promising start-ups) were made out of a total of 1,200 to 1,500 investments made. That's about 6 percent of the investments made. Since the average venture capital firm reviews 80 to 100 deals for each one they fund, the chances of getting start-up money is almost nonexistent.

We all like to ooh and ah over the exciting stories in magazines and newspapers about the money made by venture capitalists and the companies they invest in. This is where the dot.coms and bio-tech and other high-growth, glamorous companies play. If your business fits the VC's criteria, your banker, lawyer, and other investors will let you know. Otherwise, this source is not available to you.

Wisdom is the power that enables us to use knowledge for the benefit of ourselves and others.
THOMAS J. WATSON

Other businesses, including your suppliers, can help you with your financing. Suppliers offer terms, dating, and extended credit support. They want you to stay in business, and if they believe in you, they will go out of their way to help.

Networking with other business owners can steer you to other investors. You can never tell when you will come up with the right person. Ron Peterson, president of Sagamore Hill, Inc., a hotel design, development, and management firm, told Andy that he worked through more than 2,000 names before finding the right investor for his upscale Three Chimneys Inn in Durham, New Hampshire. He finally found the right investor, a graduate of the University of New Hampshire who had made it big in the entertainment industry. That's big-league networking, sometimes called "Rolodex financing."

Coming together is a beginning;
keeping together is progress;
working together is success.

HENRY FORD

Investment clubs are a possible source of patient money. While most investment clubs invest in publicly traded stocks, they may, if approached carefully, be willing to put some of their money into a local business in need of a silent investor. (A silent investor is one who provides money, stays out of management, and is patient.)

Ask your broker if there is a local investment club. If nothing else, you'll meet some interesting people, glean some investment ideas, and perhaps get your financing from one or more of the members.

We recommend that you join a charitable board for a number of reasons. Regarding the subject of small business financing, it's a great way to meet community

When Philippe Chambadal and Michael Lang, cofounders of Quadrian, a New York City start-up that makes high-end software for retrieving data, needed cash, they didn't go to a banker or a venture capitalist. They turned to Ericsson, the telecommunications giant and a potential customer for help. Ericsson grasped how Quadrian's technology could enhance software that the giant was developing called Geoportal, which allows users to access data using wireless products. So it gave the company a cash advance of $500,000 as part of a strategic licensing agreement. Once the software hits the market, both companies will share sales royalties of an undisclosed percentage. (*Fortune Small Business,* "Need Money in a Hurry?" February 2000)

leaders. Most nonprofits have professionals and people with financial know-how on their boards. They also try to get a number of community leaders whose advocacy can be helpful to you. You have a chance to show them what you can do, pick up some valuable skills, and make a contribution to your community. That's a nice trifecta. Remember the old saying: It doesn't matter who you know, it's how you are known to them.

Joining a board and being a working member of that board is a fine way to learn how to write grant proposals, a specialized form of financing proposal. We've never been on a nonprofit board that wasn't grateful for help with this central piece of work. You don't have to know how to write proposals when you begin; there's plenty of research involved that you can do to help more experienced folks concentrate on the proposal itself.

> *Where the willingness is great,*
> *the difficulties cannot be great.*
> NICCOLÒ MACHIAVELLI

Restaurants, doctors, and airline pilots go together, according to one of our academic friends who specializes in restaurant management. The reason, she says, is that "the glamour" of owning part of a restaurant overcomes the innate common sense that we hope our doctors and airline pilots have. There's something about taking friends to visit "my restaurant" and being treated as an owner. The downside is that they sometimes go too far, and insist on comping their pals, which, while fine for the ego, kills the bottom line.

Restaurants and other hospitality businesses aren't the only ones with "owner appeal," of course. Ever think of investing in a film, a play, or a dot.com? These have serious appeal that goes well beyond potential financial rewards.

While this last idea may seem odd at first, follow the logic, because many people are willing to stretch their investment boundaries in return for a tax loss. It goes like this: A Sub S corporation allows losses to pass through to the investors, a handy way to offset other income. Suppose Andi wins $50,000 at the pinochle table. She can either pay taxes on it or invest in a start-up, which, long-term, bodes to be successful, but which will almost certainly lose money for the first year. She therefore plunks $50,000 into the start-up of her choice, takes the first year loss to offset the windfall, and owns herself a chunk of a successful business. (Good job, Andi!)

Partnerships also offer this kind of pass-through benefit, but make sure that you check with your accountant to be sure that the benefit will accrue to the investors. They must be active partners, not passive.

As a side issue, accredited investors are keenly aware of the value of such tax losses, and any presentation to them might include reference to the remote chance that profits won't instantly flow.

Dwayne Walker, CEO of Seattle-based TechWave, an e-commerce service provider, invested in AccountingNet, a Seattle-based online resource for accounting information. He also became a member of its board, because the business had built a strong "vertical market" in its industry. Vertical markets are based on "peer-to-peer" selling, in which a product recommended by one professional is bought by many of his or her peers because of the recommendation. (*Inc.*, January 1999, pp. 25–28)

14

What Are Some Unconventional Sources for Financing?

If you can't get conventional financing be very wary.

Don't pay a stranger to procure money for you. Most people claiming to be able to secure financing for you—for a fee up front—will be bogus. Some will sell you lists of SBA-approved banks. Others will send you lists of names (or Web sites) of people who may or may not be in the financial world.

In your search for money, make sure to exhaust all legitimate financing alleys. If you keep being turned down, there's probably a good reason: Your business doesn't merit financing. This is not the best time to take a gamble with all of your assets. If the professionals turn you down, ask why. Listen to them, and learn.

Check with the nearest Small Business Development Center (see Appendix Two). They maintain a file of active lenders. Have you discussed your situation with your banker? Sometimes the financing won't jell because the timing is wrong or the bank is loaned up in your category. Your banker will help you understand why the bank was unable to make the loan—and may be able to steer you to another source of funds.

Richard Foos, president and founder of Rhino Records, which offers reissues of rare recordings, advises business owners to start as small as possible. "To achieve 100 percent success, you need to grow organically. Pass up outside financing until you know that you can run the company. Starting with limited financing forces you to learn every single aspect of a business: how to balance a ledger, how to collect receivables, how to draw up contracts. If you don't understand all aspects of your business, you've set yourself up to fail." (*Fast Company*, January/February 2000, p. 106)

Time and money spent in helping men to do more for themselves is far better than mere giving.
HENRY FORD

Moonlighting is a time-honored way to substitute hard work for easy financing. Many new businesses are strapped for cash to pay the owner's living expenses. Rather than spend an inordinate amount of time seeking financing, it may make sense to take on a part-time job to cover those living expenses. Andy financed an early venture this way, spending his days trying to get a start-up off the ground and three nights a week working as a Teamster (Local 25) where he made the princely sum of $2.62 an hour. (That was back in the early 1960s when a dollar had real value!)

Peer-lending groups have been around for a long time. They may be formal (such as MicroCredit New Hampshire's peer-lending groups) or informal. The common ground is that all lending decisions are made by the group, who thus acquire an understanding of the lending process from the lender's point of view. This includes setting underwriting criteria, analyzing the risk of the venture, establishing repayment schedules and terms, and collecting the debt. This is a favorite technique for immigrant families who pool their resources to back their most able relation in a venture that most of them will work in. Ever wonder how so many Chinese, Indian, Thai, and Vietnamese restaurants get funded? In earlier times such pooling of family assets was the dominant form of financing.

*He that gives should never remember,
he that receives should never forget.*
THE TALMUD

Look at your accounts receivable. If you sell a product or service to large businesses or to any government agency (local, state, or federal, it doesn't matter) you probably don't get paid before 45 to 90 days. Upstart, Andy's publishing company, once sold books to a nameless southern state university whose payment terms were end-of-semester-plus-180-days! These are good receivables, but they take so long to turn to cash to meet running expenses that they can sink a small business.

Your first step is to try to collect the receivables in a timely manner without aggravating the payables clerk. He or she has little say in when payments are made, so try to maintain your composure. If this doesn't work, see if your bank would be willing to lend against the receivables. Most banks understand the slow payment problem in which smaller businesses are essentially financing larger businesses and, if the receivables are creditworthy, will treat them as good collateral.

The next step is to see if you can find a factor to buy the receivables. Factors are a major player in industries such as clothing, where long receivables are part of the game. If you manufacture women's dresses, you sell the fall items in midwinter to stores that don't sell them for months. Factors tend to buy receivables at a steep discount (good receivables net 75 to 90 percent of face value) and add on a 2 to 6 percent discount fee. If your pricing is set up to take these costs into account (that is,

MicroCredit New Hampshire has about 170 members throughout the state in 30 business groups. One of the program's main purposes is to help finance small businesses with small loans ranging from $500 to $5,000, amounts that may not be available through a bank, especially if the business owner hasn't established a firm credit history. The local group serves as the loan-review committee; only members of the group are eligible for loans. Violeta McClellan, a Claremont, New Hampshire, woman, is looking for ways to market her patented aquarium design, and a loan from her peer-lending group could help finance her venture. (*The Eagle Times*, August 31, 1998)

if you follow industry practice) you can still make a decent profit. Factors are interested in establishing a long-term relationship with their clients, and most set a volume floor, so you will not readily find a factor if your financing needs don't meet their requirements.

Factors buy receivables either with recourse (you end up with the uncollectable receivables) or without recourse (they eat the loss). You pay substantially more for nonrecourse sale of receivables—but the factors are experts at collecting from the unwilling, and in some cases this will be a better deal for you.

Buy cheap, and sell dear.
THOMAS LODGE

If there are no factors available (because your receivables are not current or not creditworthy), it is time to turn to a collection agency. If your customers are unwilling to pay on time, they aren't worth retaining as customers; therefore the perceived insult of calling in a collection agency won't hurt you. All too often small business owners are unwilling to risk offending slow-paying customers. This is silly, since small businesses can go broke providing low-cost financing to their larger customers. You can find professional collection agencies through your chamber of commerce, accountant, or bank. Collection agencies get paid when they collect the money, so your exposure is not great. A professional collection agency will help you strengthen your internal credit and collection policies as a byproduct of their service.

He who pays the piper may call the tune.
17TH-CENTURY PROVERB

Your customers may be a source of financing. Perhaps you can induce them to pay ahead. One of our businesses provided newsletters to banks. Once we understood their budgeting cycles, we persuaded several of the largest banks to pay up-front (at a discount) for the next fiscal year. This way they got a service at a reduced price, we got some inexpensive financing, and all parties came out ahead.

If you are a key supplier, your position is even stronger: Your customer needs what you provide and has a vested interest in keeping you in business. In these days of outsourcing this is becoming a more common source of financing.

Your competition may help you out, either directly or indirectly. Remember in 1987, when American Motors, at that time the fourth-largest auto manufacturer in the United States, was going broke? General Motors and Ford helped negotiate its survival by engineering a takeover of American Motors by Chrysler, whom they wanted to remain strong enough to be a viable member of the "Big Three" automakers.

A bone to the dog is not charity.
Charity is the bone shared with the dog,
when you are just as hungry as the dog.
JACK LONDON

"In 17 years, we've turned very few overdue bills over to collection experts," explains Patty DeDominic, chief executive of PDQ Personnel Services in Los Angeles. "And we handle more than 400 corporate clients each year. We spell out our terms (payment upon receipt of a weekly invoice) before we sign up a new customer. When there's a conflict, we work out an acceptable compromise as long as the customer doesn't pose other credit risks. Then we follow up with a written document. We start to investigate once a payment is one week late. Our employees file reports of every customer contact in our database, so our staff can identify inconsistencies and failed promises. If a customer is lying to us, I'll promptly turn its bill over to a collection expert." (*Inc.*, "Get Paid Promptly," November 1996)

After 12 years in business, Patrice Wynne announced in December 1998 that she would be closing Gaia, her spiritually oriented bookstore in Berkeley, California. She attributed declining sales to Internet competition. Within days, an anonymous Berkeley resident offered to match up to $200,000 donated by other patrons. Since then, Wynne has raised more than $130,000. "Kids come in and give us their pocket change," Wynne says. "Our customers believe in people who live and work in their community. They believe in knowledgeable booksellers who are passionate about their work." Many of those who have responded to the bookstore's appeals say they have been motivated by the plight of the underdogs. (*Concord Monitor*, July 24, 1999, p. A5)

Incubators can be more than just an inexpensive place to hang out with other start-up business owners. In Cambridge, Massachusetts, a hotbed of high-tech start-ups, major investors, ranging from venture capital firms to banks and insurance companies, are pre-screening applicants and then providing not only the personal contacts, expertise, and the incubator's facilities, but also cash to those firms fortunate enough to be accepted.

There are two ways of spreading light:
to be the candle or the mirror that reflects it.
EDITH WHARTON

Research and Development (R & D) partnerships finance the time from idea or concept to production and marketing. In its most common guise, a small company with a big product idea links up with a large company that would be able to produce and market the product. The small company secures funding to research and develop the idea. The big company benefits from a new idea or technology that it might not have discovered on its own, or can ramp up the technology and bring a product to market much more rapidly than if it had to develop it from scratch. There are many products that need vast scale to be profitable. Suppose you invented a new microchip. How could you, a small business, bring this to market against Intel and other giants? You probably couldn't.

He who would learn to fly one day
must first learn to stand and walk and run
and climb and dance: one cannot fly into flying.
FRIEDRICH WILHELM NIETZSCHE

Franchises are a huge part of our economy, with more than 350,000 outlets in 75 industries. There are more than 1,500 franchisers, ranging from the familiar McDonald's and automobile dealers (yes, they are franchises, too) to very small, local franchises offering cleaning services or specialty foods. A visit to *www.franchise.org* will give you an idea of the range of franchise opportunities in the market and the many resources available to finance a franchise of your own.

Well established franchises are appealing to lenders. They have a track record that compares very favorably with other start-ups (a closure rate of under 3 percent, with most of those closing creating no monetary loss). They have well established operating procedures, which boost a new franchisee way up the learning curve. A franchise owner can draw on the accumulated experience of other persons owning the same kind of franchise, which provides a wealth of directly relevant information that is invaluable.

How costly are franchises? Eighty percent cost less than $250,000 to get up and running. The initial investments range from $5,000 on up to $500,000 and more. The good news is that if you can scrape up 30 to 35 percent of the necessary capital, you can finance the rest. There are several traditional sources for franchise financing, headed (as always) by banks and SBA 7(a) guaranteed loans (see Chapter 7, page 78). However, since many franchises require specialized buildings

Housed in an 1883 brownstone, Boston's HotBank incubator aims to provide what it calls "mentor capital" to more than a dozen young companies at a time. Each company gets its own office, furniture, computers, and phones, as well as recruiting help and access to top lawyers and accountants. Entrepreneurs will also get advice on strategy, assembling a board of directors, and pursuing the next stage of venture capital. HotBank offers up to $2 million in financing for young firms. In return, it will own 25 to 75 percent of each company. It expects protégés to sink or swim within 12 months. (*Boston Globe*, February 7, 2000, p. D6)

Douglas York purchased a Great Clips franchise in Jacksonville, Florida, with the option of opening three stores in two years as a discount package. He secured financing to open his first store by borrowing $60,000 from Textron Financial, which together with his savings of $60,000 provided sufficient funds. "You shouldn't finance yourself to the hilt," York says. "You have to leave yourself a little room to maneuver." (Entrepreneur.com's *Money, True Stories* section: "How I Got My Start-up Capital")

and/or equipment, SBA-sponsored nonbank lenders such as Certified Development Companies and Small Business Investment Companies play a major role. Suppose you have to erect a car wash—CDCs are set up to finance industrial and commercial buildings, machinery, and equipment. Equipment manufacturers themselves often provide favorable financing terms to new franchise holders. In some instances insurance and pension funds invest in franchises, especially multi-unit franchises with substantial financing needs.

Some franchisers help their franchisees with financing. In most cases this is limited to referrals to banks and other lenders who have had good experience with their business. A few will provide direct funding, though you will have to seek it out and present compelling reasons for such assistance. Almost all franchisers can help you secure equipment loans if equipment is a major part of the financing package.

Another Web site to visit for information on franchising is *www.entrepreneurmag.com*, the home page for *Entrepreneur* magazine. This site has a "franchise finder" to help you identify a franchise that is right for you and links to potential financing sources. It also— and this is where we see the most value—has what they call a "franchise toolbox." Together with the site *www.franchise.org*, this gives you access to enough material to figure out what franchise to buy and how to finance that franchise.

It is easier to add to a great reputation that to get it.
                                        PUBLIUS SYRUS

Appendix
One

Forms for Organizing Your Start-Up Costs

Use the following forms to organize your start-up costs. Not all items will apply, and you may have to add others.

Form 1: START-UP COSTS YOU ONLY HAVE TO PAY ONCE

Fixtures and equipment	$	Fill in Form 2 and put the total here
Decorating and remodeling	$	Speak with contractor
Installation of fixtures and equipment	$	Talk to suppliers
Starting inventory	$	Ask suppliers
Deposits for public utilities	$	Ask utility companies
Legal and other professional fees	$	Ask lawyer, accountant, etc.
Licenses and permits	$	Find out from city offices
Advertising and promotion for opening	$	Estimate; ask ad agencies
Accounts receivable	$	What you will need to buy more stock until credit customers pay
Cash	$	For unexpected expenses, losses, special purchases, etc.
Other (specify)	$	Make a separate list and enter total
TOTAL ESTIMATED CASH YOU NEED TO START	$	Add up all the numbers in column 1

Form 2: LIST OF FURNITURE, FIXTURES, AND EQUIPMENT

Leave out or add items to suit your business. Use separate sheets to list exactly what you need for each of the items below.	If you plan to pay cash in full, enter the full amount below and in the last column.	If you are going to pay by installments, enter in the down payment plus installments for three months.	Estimate of the cash you need for furniture, fixtures, and equipment.
Counters	$	$	$
Storage shelves, cabinets	$	$	$
Display stands, shelves, tables	$	$	$
Cash register	$	$	$
Computers and peripherals	$	$	$
Phone, fax	$	$	$
Copier	$	$	$
Safe	$	$	$
Window display fixtures	$	$	$
Special lighting	$	$	$
Outside signage	$	$	$
Delivery equipment	$	$	$
Other (specify)	$	$	$
TOTAL: Furniture, Fixtures, Equipment. Enter on Form 1 (Start-up Costs You Only Have to Pay Once)	$	$	$

Form 3: ESTIMATED MONTHLY COSTS

Item	Your estimate of monthly expenses based on sales of $_____ per year. Column 1	Your estimate of how much cash you need to start your business (see column 3). Column 2	What to put in column 2. These figures are typical for one kind of business. Column 3
Salary of owner or manager	$	$	2 times column 1
All other salaries and wages	$	$	3 times column 1
Rent or mortgage	$	$	3 times column 1
Advertising	$	$	3 times column 1
Delivery expense	$	$	3 times column 1
Supplies	$	$	3 times column 1
Telephone/fax	$	$	3 times column 1
Other utilities	$	$	3 times column 1
Insurance	$	$	Per schedule
Taxes, including FICA	$	$	4 times column 1
Interest	$	$	3 times column 1
Loan payments	$	$	3 times column 1
Maintenance	$	$	3 times column 1
Legal & other professional fees	$	$	Per schedule
Miscellaneous	$	$	3 times column 1
Other (specify)	$	$	3 times column 1
Other (specify)	$	$	3 times column 1
TOTAL MONTHLY COSTS:	$	$	

Appendix TWO

State Offices with Programs for Small Business Financing

ALABAMA
Alabama Development Office
401 Adams Avenue
Montgomery, Alabama 36104
(800) 248-0033 or (334) 242-0400
www.ado.state.al.us

SBA District Office
2121 Eighth Avenue North
Suite 200
Birmingham, Alabama 35203-2398
(205) 731-1344

Alabama Small Business
   Development Center
University of Alabama
   at Birmingham
1717 11th Avenue South, Suite 419
Birmingham, Alabama 35294
(205) 934-7260

ALASKA
Department of Commerce and
   Economic Development
State Office Building, Ninth Floor
333 Willoughby Avenue
P.O. Box 110800
Juneau, Alaska 99811-0800
(907) 465-2500
www.state.ak.us/local/business.htm

SBA District Office
222 W. Eighth Avenue,
Room A-36
Box 67
Anchorage, Alaska 99513-7559
(907) 271-4022

Alaska Small Business
   Development Center
University of Alaska at Anchorage
430 West Seventh Avenue, Suite 110
Anchorage, Alaska 99501
(907) 274-7232

ARIZONA
Arizona Business Assistance Center
Arizona Department of Commerce
3800 N. Central Avenue, Building D
Phoenix, Arizona 85012
(800) 542-5684 or (602) 280-1480
www.state.az.us/ep/

SBA District Office
2828 North Central Avenue, Suite 800
Phoenix, Arizona 85004-1093
(602) 640-2316

Arizona Small Business
   Development Center Network
2411 West 14th Street, Room 132
Tempe, Arizona 85281
(602) 731-8720

ARKANSAS
Arkansas Economic Development
   Commission
One State Capitol Mall
Little Rock, Arkansas 72201
(501) 682-1121
www.aidc.state.or.us

SBA District Office
2120 Riverfront Drive, Suite 100
Little Rock, Arkansas 72202-1747
(501) 324-5871

Arkansas Small Business
   Development Center
University of Arkansas at Little Rock
100 South Main Street, Suite 401
Little Rock, Arkansas 72201
(501) 324-9043

CALIFORNIA
California Office of Small Business
California Trade and Commerce
   Agency
801 K Street, Suite 1700
Sacramento, California 95814
(916) 324-1295
www.commerce.ca.gov

SBA District Office
660 J Street, Suite 215
Sacramento, California 95814-2413
(916) 498-6410

California Small Business
   Development Center
California Trade and Commerce
   Agency
801 K Street, Suite 1700
Sacramento, California 95814-3520
(916) 324-5068

COLORADO
Office of Business Development
1625 Broadway, Suite 1710
Denver, Colorado 80202
(303) 892-3840
www.state.co.us/gov_dir/obd/obd.htm

SBA District Office
721 19th Street, Suite 426
Denver, Colorado 80202
(303) 844-3984

Office of Business Development
Colorado Small Business
   Development Center
1625 Broadway, Suite 1710
Denver, Colorado 80202
(303) 892-3809

CONNECTICUT
Connecticut Economic Resource
   Center
805 Brook Street, Building 4
Rocky Hill, Connecticut 06067-3405
(800) 392-2122
www.cerc.com/

SBA District Office
330 Main Street, Second Floor
Hartford, Connecticut 06106
(860) 240-4700

Connecticut Small Business
   Development Center
University of Connecticut
School of Business Administration
2 Bourn Place, U-94
Storrs, Connecticut 06269-5094
(860) 486-4135

DELAWARE
Delaware Economic Development
   Office
99 Kings Highway
P.O. Box 1401
Dover, Delaware 19903
(302) 739-4271
www.state.de.us/dedo/index.htm

SBA District Office
824 North Market Street, Suite 610
Wilmington, Delaware 19899
(302) 573-6294

Delaware Small Business
Development Center
University of Delaware
Purnell Hall, Suite 005
Newark, Delaware 19716-2711
(800) 222-2279 or (302) 831-1555

DISTRICT OF COLUMBIA
Office of the Assistant City
  Administrator for Economic
  Development
441 4th Street, NW, Suite 1140
Washington, D.C. 20001
(202) 727-6365
www.ci.washingtondc.us/

SBA District Office
1110 Vermont Avenue, NW, Suite 900
P.O. Box 34500
Washington, D.C. 20043
(202) 606-4000

Metropolitan Washington Small
  Business Development Center
Howard University
2600 Sixth Street, NW, Room 125
Washington, D.C. 20059
(202) 806-1550

FLORIDA
Enterprise Florida
390 N. Orange Avenue, Suite 1300
Orlando, Florida 32801
(407) 316-4600
www.floridabusiness.com/

SBA District Office
100 South Biscayne Blvd.,
Seventh Floor
Miami, Florida 33131
(305) 536-5521

Florida Small Business
  Development Center
University of West Florida
19 West Garden Street, Suite 300
Pensacola, Florida 32501
(850) 595-6060

GEORGIA
Georgia Department of Industry,
  Trade and Tourism
P.O. Box 1776
Atlanta, Georgia 30301
(404) 656-3545
www.gditt.com

SBA District Office
1720 Peachtree Road, NW, Suite 600
Atlanta, Georgia 30309
(404) 347-4749

University of Georgia
Business Outreach Services,
Chicopee Complex
1180 East Broad Street
Athens, Georgia 30602-5412
(404) 542-6762

HAWAII
Business Action Center
1130 North Nimitz Hwy., Suite A-254
Honolulu, Hawaii 96817-4580
(808) 586-2545
www.hawaii.gov/dbedt/

SBA District Office
300 Ala Moana Boulevard, 2-235
Box 50207
Honolulu, Hawaii 96850-4981
(808) 541-2990

Hawaii Small Business
  Development Center
University of Hawaii at Hilo
200 West Kawili Street
Hilo, Hawaii 96720-4091
(808) 974-7515

IDAHO
Department of Commerce
700 West State Street
P.O. Box 83720
Boise, Idaho 83720-0093
(208) 334-2470
www.idoc.state.id.us/pages/
  BUSINESSPAGE.html

SBA District Office
1020 Main Street, Suite 290
Boise, Idaho 83702-5745
(208) 334-1696

Idaho Small Business
  Development Center
Boise State University
College of Business
1910 University Drive
Boise, Idaho 83725
(800) 225-3815 or (208) 385-1640

ILLINOIS
Department of Commerce and
  Community Affairs
620 East Adams Street, Third Floor
Springfield, Illinois 62701
(217) 524-5856
www.commerce.state.il.us

SBA District Office
511 West Capitol Avenue, Suite 302
Springfield, Illinois 62704
(217) 492-4416

Illinois Small Business
  Development Center
Department of Commerce
  & Community Affairs
620 East Adams Street, Third Floor
Springfield, Illinois 62701
(217) 524-5856

INDIANA
State Information Center
402 West Washington Street,
Room W160
Indianapolis, Indiana 46204
(317) 233-0800
www.ai.org.bdev/index/html

SBA District Office
429 North Pennsylvania Street,
Suite 100
Indianapolis, Indiana 46204-1873
(317) 226-7272

Indiana Small Business
    Development Center
One North Capitol, Suite 420
Indianapolis, Indiana 46204-2248
(317) 264-6871

IOWA
Department of Economic Development
200 East Grand Avenue
Des Moines, Iowa 50309
(515) 242-4700
www.state.ia.us/government/ided

SBA District Office
210 Walnut Street, Room 749
Des Moines, Iowa 50309-2186
(515) 284-4422

Iowa Small Business
    Development Center
Iowa State University
College of Business Administration
137 Lynn Avenue
Ames, Iowa 50014-7126
(800) 373-7232 or (515) 292-6351

KANSAS
Department of Commerce
    and Housing
700 SW Harrison Street, Suite 1300
Topeka, Kansas 66603-3712
(785) 296-3481
www.kansascommerce.com

SBA District Office
100 East English Street, Suite 510
Wichita, Kansas 67202
(316) 269-6616

Kansas Small Business
    Development Center
Wichita State University
1845 Fairmount
Wichita, Kansas 67260-0148
(316) 978-3193

KENTUCKY
Kentucky Cabinet for Economic
    Development
2300 Capital Plaza Tower
Frankfort, Kentucky 40601
(502) 564-7670
www.state.ky.us/edc/cabmain.htm

SBA District Office
600 Dr. M. L. King, Jr. Place,
Room 188
Louisville, Kentucky 40202
(502) 582-5971

Kentucky Small Business
    Development Center
University of Kentucky
Center for Business Development
225 Business and Economics Building
Lexington, Kentucky 40506-0034
(606) 257-7668

LOUISIANA
Department of Economic
  Development
P.O. Box 94185
Baton Rouge, Louisiana 70804-9185
(504) 342-3000
www.lded.state.la.us

SBA District Office
365 Canal Street, Suite 2250
New Orleans, Louisiana 70130
(504) 589-2354

Louisiana Small Business
  Development Center
Northeast Louisiana University
College of Business Administration,
Room 2-57
Monroe, Louisiana 71209-6435
(318) 342-5506

MAINE
Department of Economic
  and Community Development
State House Station #59
Augusta, Maine 04333-0059
(800) 541-5872
or (800) 872-3838 (in-state)
www.econdevmaine.com/

SBA District Office
40 Western Avenue, Room 512
Augusta, Maine 04330
(207) 622-8378

Maine Small Business
  Development Center
University of Southern Maine
93 Falmouth Street, P.O. Box 9300
Portland, Maine 04104-9300
(207) 780-4420

MARYLAND
Department of Business and
  Economic Development
Redwood Tower
217 East Redwood Street
Baltimore, Maryland 21202
(410) 767-6300
www.dbed.state.md.us/

SBA District Office
10 South Howard Street, Suite 6220
Baltimore, Maryland 21201
(410) 962-4392

Maryland Small Business
  Development Center
7100 Baltimore Avenue, Suite 401
College Park, MD 20740
(301) 403-8300

MASSACHUSETTS
Department of Economic Development
One Ashburton Place, Room 2101
Boston, Massachusetts 02108
(617) 727-8380
www.magnet.state.ma.us/mobd

SBA District Office
10 Causeway Street, Room 265
Boston, Massachusetts 02222-1093
(617) 565-5590

Massachusetts Small Business
   Development Center
University of Massachusetts
School of Management, Room 205
Amherst, Massachusetts 01003
(413) 545-6301

MICHIGAN
Michigan Jobs Commission
Victor Office Center, Fourth Floor
210 N. Washington Square
Lansing, Michigan 48913
(517) 373-9808
www.mjc.state.mi.us

SBA District Office
477 Michigan Avenue, Room 515
Detroit, Michigan 48226
(313) 226-6075

Michigan Small Business
   Development Center
Wayne State University
2727 Second Avenue, Room 107
Detroit, Michigan 48201
(313) 964-1798

MINNESOTA
Small Business Assistance Office
500 Metro Square
121 7th Place East
St. Paul, Minnesota 55101-2146
(800) 657-3858
www.dted.state.mn.us/busasst/html

SBA District Office
100 North Sixth Street, Suite 610-C
Minneapolis, Minnesota 55403-1563
(612) 370-2324

Minnesota Small Business
   Development Center
Department of Trade and Economic
   Development
Small Business Assistance Office
500 Metro Square
121 7th Place East
St. Paul, Minnesota 55101-2146
(612) 297-5770

MISSISSIPPI
Mississippi Department of Economic
   and Community Development
P.O. Box 849
Jackson, Mississippi 39205-0849
(601) 359-3349
www.decd.state.ms.us

SBA District Office
100 West Capitol Street, Suite 400
Jackson, Mississippi 39201
(601) 965-4378

Mississippi Small Business
  Development Center
University of Mississippi
Old Chemistry Building, Suite 216
University, Mississippi 38677
(601) 232-5001

MISSOURI
Missouri Department of
  Economic Development
Truman State Office Building
301 West High Street, Room 680, P.O.
Box 1157
Jefferson City, Missouri 65102
(800) 523-1434 or (573) 751-4962
www.ecodev.state.mo.us

SBA District Office
Lucas Place
323 West Eighth Street, Suite 501
Kansas City, Missouri 64105
(816) 374-6708

Missouri Small Business
  Development Center
University of Missouri
300 University Place
Columbia, Missouri 65211
(573) 882-0344

MONTANA
Department of Commerce
1424 Ninth Avenue
Helena, Montana 59620-0501
(406) 444-3494
commerce.mt.gov

SBA District Office
301 South Park, Drawer 10054,
Room 334
Helena, Montana 59626
(406) 441-1081

Montana Small Business
  Development Center
Montana Department of Commerce
1424 Ninth Avenue
Helena, Montana 59620
(406) 444-4780

NEBRASKA
Nebraska Department of Economic
  Development
P.O. Box 94666,
301 Centennial Mall South
Lincoln, Nebraska 68509-4666
(800) 426-6505
www.ded.state.ne.us

SBA District Office
11145 Mill Valley Road
Omaha, Nebraska 68154
(402) 221-4691

Nebraska Small Business
   Development Center
University of Nebraska at Omaha
College of Business Administration
   Building
60th and Dodge Streets, Room 407
Omaha, Nebraska 68182
(402) 554-2521

NEVADA
Nevada State Development
   Corporation
350 South Center Street, Room 310
Reno, Nevada 89501
(702) 323-3625
www.state.ne.us

SBA District Office
301 E. Stewart Street, Room 301
P.O. Box 7527
Las Vegas, Nevada 89125-2527
(702) 388-6611

Nevada Small Business
   Development Center
University of Nevada at Reno
College of Business Administration
Mail Stop 032
1664 North Virginia Street
Reno, Nevada 89503
(702) 784-1717

NEW HAMPSHIRE
Business Finance Authority
New Hampshire Industrial
   Development Authority
14 Dixon Avenue, Suite 101
Concord, New Hampshire 03301-4954
(603) 271-2391
www.state.nh.us/bfa/bfa.htm

SBA District Office
143 North Main Street, Suite 202
P.O. Box 1258
Concord, New Hampshire 03302-1257
(603) 225-1400

New Hampshire Small Business
   Development Center
University of New Hampshire
108 McConnell Hall
Durham, New Hampshire 03824
(603) 862-2200

NEW JERSEY
New Jersey Department of Commerce
   and Economic Development
20 West State Street
CN 835
Trenton, New Jersey 08625
(609) 292-2444
www.njeda.com/

SBA District Office
2 Gateway Center, Fourth Floor
Newark, New Jersey 07102
(973) 645-2434

New Jersey Small Business
  Development Center
Rutgers University
Graduate School of Management,
  University Heights
180 University Avenue
Newark, New Jersey 07102
(973) 648-5950

NEW MEXICO
Economic Development Department
P.O. Box 20003
Santa Fe, New Mexico 87504-5003
(505) 827-0300
www.edd.state.nm.us/

SBA District Office
625 Silver Avenue, SW, Suite 320
Albuquerque, New Mexico 87102
(505) 766-1870

New Mexico Small Business
  Development Center
Santa Fe Community College
P.O. Box 4187
South Richards Avenue
Santa Fe, New Mexico 87502-4187
(505) 428-1362

NEW YORK
Empire State Development
633 Third Avenue
New York, New York 10017
(212) 803-2319
www.empire.state.ny.us/

SBA District Office
26 Federal Plaza, Room 3100
New York, New York 10278
(212) 264-4355

New York Small Business
  Development Center
State University of New York (SUNY)
SUNY Plaza S-523
Albany, New York 12246
(518) 433-5398 or (800) 732-SBDC

NORTH CAROLINA
North Carolina Small Business and
  Technology Development Center
333 Fayetteville Street Mall,
Suite 1150
Raleigh, North Carolina 26701
(919) 715-7272
www.sbtdc.org

SBA District Office
200 North College Street, Suite A2015
Charlotte, North Carolina 28202-2173
(704) 344-3563

NORTH DAKOTA
Department of Economic
   Development and Finance
1833 East Bismarck Expressway
Bismarck, North Dakota 58504
(701) 328-5300
www.growingnd.com/

SBA District Office
657 Second Avenue North, Room 219
P.O. Box 3086
Fargo, North Dakota 58108-3086
(701) 239-5131

North Dakota Small Business
   Development Center
University of North Dakota
118 Gamble Hall
Grand Forks, North Dakota 58202-7308
(701) 777-3700

OHIO
Office of Small and
   Developing Business
Ohio Department of Development
77 South High Street
P.O. Box 1001
Columbus, Ohio 43216-1001
(614) 466-2718
www.odod.ohio.gov/

SBA District Office
2 Nationwide Plaza, Suite 1400
Columbus, Ohio 43215
(513) 469-6860

Ohio Small Business Development
   Center
Ohio Department of Development
77 South High Street
P.O. Box 1001
Columbus, Ohio 43216-1001
(614) 466-2711

OKLAHOMA
Oklahoma Department
   of Commerce
900 North Stiles, P.O. Box 26980
Oklahoma City, Oklahoma 73126-0980
(800) 879-6552 or (405) 815-6552
www.odoc.state.ok.us

SBA District Office
210 Park Avenue, Suite 1300
Oklahoma City, Oklahoma 73102
(405) 231-5521

Oklahoma Small Business
   Development Center
Southeastern State University
517 West University
Durant, Oklahoma 74730
(580) 924-0277 or (800) 522-6154

OREGON
Economic Development Office
775 Summer Street, NE
Salem, Oregon 97310
(503) 986-0123
www.econ.state.or.us

SBA District Office
1515 SW 15th Avenue, Suite 1050
Portland, Oregon 97201-6695
(503) 326-2682

Oregon Small Business
  Development Center
Lane Community College
44 West Broadway, Suite 501
Eugene, Oregon 97401-3021
(541) 726-2250

PENNSYLVANIA
Small Business Resource Center
Department of Community and
  Economic Development
374 Forum Building
Harrisburg, Pennsylvania 17120
(800) 280-3801
www.teampa.com

SBA District Office
100 Chestnut Street, Suite 108
Harrisburg, Pennsylvania 17101
(717) 782-3840

Pennsylvania Small Business
  Development Center
University of Pennsylvania,
  The Wharton School
Vance Hall, 4th Floor
3733 Spruce Street
Philadelphia, Pennsylvania 19104-6374
(215) 898-1219

PUERTO RICO
Economic Development
  Administration
355 F. D. Roosevelt Avenue
Hato Rey, Puerto Rico 00918-2318
(787) 758-4747
www.pr-eda.com/econ-dev.html

SBA District Office
Citibank Building
252 Ponce de Leon Avenue,
Plaza Level
Hato Rey, Puerto Rico 00918
(787) 766-5572

RHODE ISLAND
Rhode Island Economic
  Development Corporation
One West Exchange Street
Providence, Rhode Island 02903
(401) 222-2601
www.riedc.com

SBA District Office
380 Westminster Street
Providence, Rhode Island 02903
(401) 528-4561

Rhode Island Small Business
   Development Center
Bryant College Small Business
Development Center
1150 Douglas Pike
Smithfield, Rhode Island 02917-1282
(401) 232-6111

SOUTH CAROLINA
Enterprise Development, Inc.
P.O. Box 11490
Columbia, South Carolina 29202
(803) 252-8806
www.state.sc.us/commerce

SBA District Office
1835 Assembly Street, Room 358
Columbia, South Carolina 29201
(803) 765-5376

South Carolina Small Business
   Development Center
University of South Carolina
College of Business Administration
Columbia, South Carolina 29208
(803) 829-1040

SOUTH DAKOTA
Governor's Office of Economic
   Development
711 East Wells Avenue
Pierre, South Dakota 57501-3369
(800) 872-6190
www.state.sd.us/stateexecutive/oed/oed.htm

SBA District Office
110 South Phillips, Suite 200
Sioux Falls, South Dakota 57104-6727
(605) 330-4231

South Dakota Small Business
   Development Center
University of South Dakota,
   School of Business
Patterson Hall 115
414 East Clarke Street
Vermillion, South Dakota 57069
(605) 677-5498

TENNESSEE
Department of Economic
   and Community Development
320 Sixth Avenue North
Nashville, Tennessee 37243
(800) 342-8470 (in state)
or (800) 251-8594
www.tnedc.org/

SBA District Office
50 Vantage Way, Suite 201
Nashville, Tennessee 37228-1500
(615) 736-5881

Tennessee Small Business
  Development Center
University of Memphis
South Campus, Getwell Road,
Building #1
Memphis, Tennessee 38152
(901) 678-2500

TEXAS
Texas Department of Economic
  Development
1700 North Congress Avenue
P.O. Box 12728
Austin, Texas 78711
(512) 936-0100
www.tded.state.tx.us

SBA District Office
606 N. Carancahua, Suite 1200
Corpus Christi, Texas 78476
(512) 888-3331

Texas Small Business
  Development Center
Dallas County Community College
1402 Corinth Street, Suite 2111
Dallas, Texas 75215
(214) 860-5831

UTAH
Division of Business and Economic
  Development
324 South State Street, Suite 500
Salt Lake City, Utah 84111
(801) 538-8700
www.dced.state.ut.us/dbed/welcome.htm

SBA District Office
125 South State Street, Room 2237
Salt Lake City, Utah 84138-1195
(801) 524-3209

Utah Small Business
  Development Center
University of Utah
8811 South 700 East
Sandy, Utah 84070
(435) 255-5991

VERMONT
Business Development,
  Expansion and Recruitment
Vermont Department of Economic
  Development
109 State Street
Montpelier, Vermont 05602
(802) 828-3211
*www.state.vt.us/dca/economic/
  developm.htm*

SBA District Office
87 State Street, Room 205
P.O. Box 605
Montpelier, Vermont 05601
(802) 828-4422

Vermont Small Business
   Development Center
Vermont Technical College
P.O. Box 422
Randolph, Vermont 05060-0422
(802) 728-9101 or (800) 464-SBDC

VIRGINIA
Virginia Department of Business
   Assistance
P.O. Box 798
Richmond, Virginia 23218-0798
(804) 371-8200
www.vdba.org/

SBA District Office
1504 Santa Rosa Road, Suite 200
Richmond, Virginia 23229
(804) 771-2400

Virginia Small Business
   Development Center
Commonwealth of Virginia
   Department of Economic
   Development
Virginia Business Development
   Network
901 East Byrd Street, West Tower,
19th Floor
Richmond, Virginia 23206
(804) 371-8253

WASHINGTON
Business Assistance Center
Department of Community,
   Trade and Economic Development
906 Columbia Street SW
P.O. Box 48300
Olympia, Washington 98504-8300
(360) 753-4900
www.wa.gov/cted/

SBA District Office
1200 6th Avenue, Suite 1700
Seattle, Washington 98101-1128
(206) 553-7310

Washington Small Business
   Development Center
Washington State University
Johnson Tower 501
Pullman, Washington 99164-4851
(509) 335-1576

WEST VIRGINIA
West Virginia Development Office
West Virginia Economic
   Development Authority
1018 Kanawha Boulevard East,
Suite 501
Charleston, West Virginia 25301
(304) 558-3650
www.wvdo.org

SBA District Office
405 Capitol Street, Suite 412
Charleston, West Virginia 25301
(304) 347-5220

West Virginia Small Business
   Development Center
West Virginia Development Office
950 Kanawha Boulevard East,
Suite 501
Charleston, West Virginia 25301
(304) 558-2960

WISCONSIN
Department of Development
201 West Washington Avenue
P.O. Box 7970
Madison, Wisconsin 53703
(608) 266-1018 or (800) 435-7287
badger.state.wi.us/agencies/dod

SBA District Office
212 East Washington Avenue,
Room 213
Madison, Wisconsin 53703
(608) 264-5261

Wisconsin Small Business
   Development Center
University of Wisconsin
432 North Lake Street, Room 423
Madison, Wisconsin 53706
(608) 263-7794

WYOMING
Division of Economic and
   Community Development
Herschler Building 1EW
122 West 25th Street
Cheyenne, Wyoming 82002
(307) 777-7284
commerce.state.wy.us/decd/index/htm

SBA District Office
100 East B Street
Federal Building, Room 4001
P.O. Box 2839
Casper, Wyoming 82602-2839
(307) 261-6500

Wyoming Small Business
   Development Center
University of Wyoming
P.O. Box 3622
Laramie, Wyoming 82071-3622
(307) 766-3505 or (800) 348-5194

Appendix Three

Financial Ratios

Bankers and other investors use *ratio analysis*, a tool that helps them determine how well you are managing your business and what risks their investment might run into. If your Current Ratio, Acid Test, or Debt/Worth are out of whack with your banker's expectations, you have some serious explaining to do. This appendix is a brief introduction to ratio analysis—fuller treatment can be found in any standard finance textbook. Since banks are such an important financing source for small businesses, we concentrate on a handful of ratios of particular interest to bankers.

If you understand how to use ratio analysis you gain more than insights into the investment decision process. Ratios can alert you to developing trends, both good and bad, help you forecast the effect of operations and financing on your profitability, and in general assist you in tightening up cash management.

Ratios are used *absolutely*, standing on their own as measures of your business at the time the information they are based on was compiled. The dates of the statements are important: a merchant stocking up for holiday sales will have a lot of inventory in November, very little in January. He may also show profits in January, though not in December.

Ratios also are used *relatively*, comparing performance to trade or industry standards (Robert Morris Associates and others), to historic performance, or to other standards. Both uses are valuable. Make sure that you compare apples to apples, though. One of the concerns we have about RMA figures is that they are based on a number of large companies with well established patterns, whereas a small business may be brand new—and in any case won't have the stable patterns of a bigger business.

Keeping track of key ratios over a period of months or years is a powerful way to spot trends in the making. Some of the operating ratios (see pages 199–200) are particularly useful if charted. You might even consider posting the changes in these ratios as the months go by. It helps your employees understand how the company's finances work.

Ratios are commonly categorized in four groups: Liquidity, Coverage, Leverage, and Operating.

To illustrate how ratios are calculated (and to give a sense of how they are used), refer to the examples of financial statements on page 201.

A. Liquidity Ratios
    Liquidity ratios indicate your company's ability to meet current obligations on time. An illiquid firm has difficulty paying its bills and needs more capital, better management, or both.

    1. Current Ratio = $\dfrac{\text{Total Current Assets}}{\text{Total Current Liabilities}}$

    Example of Current Ratio: $\dfrac{\$74,500}{\$26,000} = 2.9$

        The current ratio is used to measure ability to meet short-term debt. The rule of thumb is that this should be at least 2:1. This is because some of the assets involved (especially inventories) will take awhile to turn to cash. The current ratio is dependent upon the quality of the current assets—if the receivables are old or uncollectable, the current ratio is misleading.

        The current ratio is the most widely used single ratio. Its widespread use highlights the importance of maintaining liquidity.

2.   Acid Test (or Quick Ratio)

$$= \frac{\text{Cash} + \text{Equivalents} + \text{Accounts Receivable}}{\text{Total Current Liabilities}}$$

Example of Acid Test: $\frac{\$41,500}{\$26,000} = 1.6$

This is a more precise measure of current liquidity. The rule of thumb calls for an acid-test ratio of 1:1. A ratio lower than 1:1 indicates an unhealthy reliance on inventory or other current assets to meet short-term obligations. A higher acid-test ratio may indicate excessive cash or lax collection efforts. Remember that the quality of the assets (receivables in particular) is important though not easily measured.

3.   Sales/Receivables $= \dfrac{\text{Net Sales}}{\text{Accounts Receivable (Net)}}$

Example of Sales/Receivables: $\dfrac{\$356,000}{\$33,000} = 10.8$

This ratio measures the annual turnover of receivables. Higher values indicate a shorter term between sales and cash collection. Lower values can indicate a collection problem due either to lax collection efforts or low-quality receivables. Track this one carefully; the changes are revealing.

4.   Days' Receivables $= \dfrac{365}{\text{Sales/Receivables}}$

Example of Days' Receivables: $\dfrac{365}{10.8} = 34$ days

This measures the average time in days that accounts receivable are outstanding. If your terms are net 30, this figure will (or should) be 30 or less.

5. Cost of Sales/Inventory = $\dfrac{\text{Cost of Sales}}{\text{Inventory}}$

Example of Cost of Sales/Inventory:

Cost of Sales = 38% of sales = $356,000 times 38% = $135,000
Average Inventory = $30,000

Cost of Sales/Inventory = $\dfrac{\$135,000}{\$30,000}$ = 4.5

Use an average inventory figure rather than year-end or a similar unusual figure to avoid distortion by a heavy year-end inventory figure. The average inventory will give you a truer picture of how your business is actually doing over the course of the year.

Days' Inventory = $\dfrac{365}{\text{Cost of Sales/Inventory}}$

$= \dfrac{365}{4.5}$ = 81 days' inventory

This ratio is affected by your inventory cycle. It should average down to 45 days. This ratio measures how frequently you turn your inventory. Higher is generally better, but an abnormally high or low ratio relative to industry figures is a danger sign. Too high a figure is usually caused by either overtrading or inability to maintain adequate inventories, a result of undercapitalization. This ratio doesn't take seasonal fluctuations into account. Cost of sales is used instead of net sales to eliminate imbalances caused by profit margins. (Days' inventory is calculated by 365 divided by Cost of Sales/Inventory.)

6. Cost of Sales/Payables = $\dfrac{\text{Cost of Sales}}{\text{Trade Payables}}$

This ratio measures annual turnover of trade payables. Higher values indicate a shorter time between purchase and payment. Generally lower numbers, down to the industry standard, indicate good performance. Below industry standards ("leaning on trade") can indicate liquidity problems. This ratio doesn't take seasonality into account.

Example of Cost of Sales/Payables: $\dfrac{\$135,000}{\$15,000} = 9$

$$\text{Days' Payables} = \frac{365}{\text{Cost of Sales/}\atop\text{Payables}} = \frac{365}{9} = 41 \text{ days}$$

7. Sales/Working Capital $= \dfrac{\text{Net Sales}}{\text{Net Working Capital}}$

Example of Sales/Working Capital: $\dfrac{356,000}{49,000} = 7.3$

Working capital is calculated by subtracting current liabilities from current assets. This ratio measures the margin of protection for current creditors and reflects the ability to finance current operations, and also measures how efficiently working capital is employed. A low value indicates inefficient use of working capital, while a high ratio indicates a vulnerable position for creditors.

B. Coverage Ratios
Coverage ratios measure the company's ability to service debt, particularly bank debt. Bankers and other creditors look at these ratios very closely.

8. EBIT/Interest $= \dfrac{\text{Earnings Before Interest} + \text{Taxes}}{\text{Annual Interest Expense}}$

Example of EBIT/Interest: $\dfrac{\$28,500}{\$3,500} = 8.1$

This measures ability to meet interest payments. In general, a higher ratio indicates a favorable capacity to take on additional debt.

C. Leverage Ratios

Leverage ratios measure exposure to risk and vulnerability to business downturns. The higher the leverage, the higher the risk, and the higher the potential profits. These ratios are looked at closely by bankers, especially if the credit is not 100 percent secured by good collateral. Remember that bankers are by nature averse to risk.

9. Fixed/Worth $= \dfrac{\text{Net Fixed Assets}}{\text{Tangible Net Worth}}$

Example of Fixed/Worth: $\dfrac{\$22,500}{\$51,000} = 0.44$

This ratio measures the extent to which owner's equity has been invested in plant and equipment. For creditors, the lower the ratio the better. Note that the assets are net of depreciation and that Tangible Net Worth washes intangibles (such as goodwill) off the books. Substantial leased assets may artificially and deceptively lower this ratio, which has been offered as a specious and potentially dangerous reason to lease plant and equipment rather than to buy it.

10. Debt/Worth $= \dfrac{\text{Total Liabilities}}{\text{Tangible Net Worth}}$

Example of Debt/Worth: $\dfrac{\$46,000}{\$51,000} = 0.9$

Every banker looks at this measure of the relationship between debt and ownership. High ratios scare creditors, whereas low ratios may indicate excessive and unprofitable caution. Ask your banker what he or she would like this to be for a firm such as yours. If the answer doesn't make sense to you, explain why your ratio is whatever it is.

D. Operating Ratios

Operating ratios measure management performance. Comparing these ratios across time is one indicator of efficient management, subject to the usual "all things being equal" reservation. Think of these as batting averages for management, most meaningful when contrasted with those of other businesses.

11. Percent Profit Before Taxes/Net Worth $= \dfrac{\text{Profit Before Taxes}}{\text{Tangible Net Worth}} \times 100$

This is another ratio where very high or very low numbers indicate possible problems. A high ratio can mean that you are doing a great job. It could also mean that you are undercapitalized. A low value could be the result of overly conservative management of a well capitalized company.

Example of Percent Profit Before Taxes/Net Worth:

$$\dfrac{\$32,000}{\$51,000} \times 100 = 63\%$$

This indicates possible undercapitalization. More capital would lower the ratio to a more acceptable level.

12. Percent Profit Before Taxes/Total Assets $= \dfrac{\text{Profit Before Taxes}}{\text{Total Assets}} \times 100$

This uses pretax profit to eliminate the vagaries of taxation. The higher the better, though it can be distorted by heavily depreciated assets, sizable intangible assets, or unusual income or expense items.

Example of Percent Profit Before Taxes/Total Assets:

$$\frac{\$32,000}{\$97,000} \; x \; 100 = 33\%$$

13. Sales/Net Fixed Assets $= \dfrac{\text{Net Sales}}{\text{Net Fixed Assets}}$

This ratio measures the productive use of fixed assets. It also can be used, in conjunction with the next ratio and others, to estimate capital needs and how assets should be allocated in a start-up.

Example of Sales/Net Fixed Assets: $\dfrac{\$356,000}{\$22,500} = 15.8$

14. Sales/Total Assets $= \dfrac{\text{Net Sales}}{\text{Total Assets}}$

This ratio measures ability to generate sales in relation to total assets. Low assets or unusual sales patterns such as a start-up exhibits will affect it.

Example of Sales/Total Assets: $\dfrac{\$356,000}{\$97,000} = 3.7$

15. Sales/Employees $= \dfrac{\text{Total Sales}}{\text{Number of Employees}}$

This measures how well a business is using its employees, and is often used as a comparative measure. A higher figure indicates better equipment, higher productivity, or better personnel management. Or all three.

Balance Sheet Worksheet: 12/31/01

Assets		Liabilities	
Cash	$8,500	Accounts payable	$15,000
Accounts receivable	$33,000	Current portion long-term debt	$5,400
Inventory	$30,000	Notes payable	$2,000
Prepaid expenses	$2,000	Accrued expenses	$2,400
Other	$1,000	Income tax payable	$0
Total: Current Assets	$74,500	Other current liabilities	$1,200
Fixtures	$6,500	**Total: Current Liabilities**	$26,000
Equipment	$18,000	Notes payable (long-term)	$0
Leasehold improvements	$10,000	Bank loans payable	$8,000
Buildings	$0	Deferred taxes	$0
Land	$0	Other loans payable	$12,000
Accumulated depreciation	–$12,000	Other long-term liabilities	$0
Intangibles	$0	**Total: Long-term Liabilities**	$20,000
Other fixed assets	$0	**Total: Liabilities**	$46,000
Total: Fixed Assets	$22,500	Retained earnings	$25,000
Total: Assets	$97,000	Invested capital	$26,000
		Other	$0
		Total: Net Worth	$51,000
		Total: Liabilities & Net Worth	$97,000

P&L Worksheet—year ending 12/31/01

Sales	$356,000	**Sales**	$356,000
Cost of sales	$135,280	**Cost of sales**	$135,000
(38%)		**Gross margin**	$221,000
EBIT	$28,500	**Operating**	
Profit before taxes	$32,000	**expenses:**	
		Salaries	$135,000
		Marketing &	$32,500
		advertising	
		Other operating	$18,000
		expenses	
		Interest expense	$3,500
		Total: Operating	$189,000
		Expenses	
		Pretax Profit (Loss)	$32,000
		EBIT	
		Federal taxes	$28,500
		State taxes	$0
		Net profit (loss)	$1,200
			$30,800

Appendix Four

Resources on the Internet

allbusiness.com bunches individual providers of accounting, payroll, consulting, software services, etc., and sells them to small businesses. The site offers more than 300 downloadable business forms, from simple legal forms to sexual harassment policy forms. But like most small business sites that offer services, allbusiness.com takes a cut of what you pay to providers.

americanexpress.com/smallbusiness is an easy-to-navigate site that offers timely small business news and advice on a range of topics, from financing to firing an employee. There's also an abundance of information on AmEx services like corporate cards and equipment financing. Surfers are able to pose questions to experts, whose creden-

tials are prominently displayed, and actually receive replies. However, be prepared for lots of distracting ads for American Express services.

bargaindog.com fetches the best e-commerce deals by employing professional shoppers to find items selling for rock-bottom prices.

bizbot.net is an online business directory that lets you easily search by business topics, such as advertising, e-commerce, and Web-site design, without getting sent to hundreds of irrelevant sites.

bizbuyer.com functions as an Ebay for business services, matching buyers and sellers of products and services—everything from sport utility vehicles to system integration to translation services. Small businesses can browse and request quotes for the services offered. They can also use the site as a seller and, for a percentage fee, post their services for sale on the site.

businessfinance.com contains valuable content about accounts receivable financing, angel investors, business-friendly banks, cash-flow management, direct public offerings, equipment leasing, micro loans, seed capital, venture capitalists, and more.

entrepreneurmag.com comes to you courtesy of *Entrepreneur* magazine. Some of their material is insultingly simpleminded but don't be deterred. They have some gems, especially in vignettes of real small business predicaments and solutions. They are particularly good on franchising and maintain an updated and easily accessible listing of franchises of all sorts.

entreworld.com is funded by the Kauffman Center for Entrepreneurial Leadership, and its search engine can scan more than 800 sites for articles on a variety of topics—pricing, franchising, financing. It also offers its own articles, including a series by successful entrepreneurs on different topics each month.

ernie.ey.com is Ernst & Young's LLP's Web-based consulting service, which lets you e-mail questions to appropriate experts, who reply in two business days. You can also tap into Ernie's growing database of previously asked questions, as well as into a trend-watching page that posts commonly asked questions by industry. But the service is pricey; $3,500 gives you answers to 10 questions a year while $18,000 buys unlimited access.

expertmarketplace.com includes a database of more than 214,000 consulting firms, along with articles and case studies.

Forbes.com provides weekly coverage of technology start-ups, the venture capital business, and tips for small business. Also available is a complete archive of *Forbes* magazine's Up and Comers and Start Your Own Business sections and an interactive version of the annual 200 Best Small Companies list.

ftc.gov belongs to the Federal Trade Commission and provides the latest on consumer protection and fraud issues, information on franchises and business opportunities, details on antitrust and competition cases, and more.

Garage.com offers services, forums, and updated news for entrepreneurs seeking seed capital from $1 million to $4 million. The Web site is the brainchild of Guy Kawasaki, former Apple evangelist, and his band of angel investors, which include high-net-worth individuals, angel groups, and a few of the venture-capital "gods" of Menlo Park's famed Sand Hill Road.

homeofficemag.com features articles on running a home-based business and is a "must-read" e-zine for anyone working from home.

Ideacafe.com bills itself as "The Small Business Channel: A fun approach to serious business." They offer the usual books, forms, and so forth—and also interactive chat rooms where you can exchange ideas with other small business folks. Their finance site (access through their home page) is worth a visit.

Kiplinger.com has a fine small business section. *Kiplinger's* is the excellent personal finance magazine, so the high standards represented on this site come as no surprise.

LendingTree.com calls itself a "loan resource center" and works with par-ticipating lenders to help consumers find the appropriate mortgage, home-equity loan, auto loan, or personal loan. Consumers can also get information on debt consolidation, refinancing, and credit reports.

microsoft.com/smallbiz offers solid technical information on creating Web sites and finding the right tech consultant. There are some useful stories on issues like e-commerce and workplace productivity, but be aware that most of them are thinly veiled attempts by Microsoft to advertise its products.

sba.gov, of the U.S. Small Business Administration, offers solid basic information about starting, financing, and expanding a business. The site also includes links to state home pages and to federal agencies, referrals to local SBA chapters and affiliates, and information on SBA loans and assistance programs. Its ACE-Net service matches investors and entrepreneurs, while PRO-Net connects business owners to business services.

score.org, the Web site of the Service Corps of Retired Executives, offers articles, workshop information, and links to other sites, along with e-mail counsel for start-up ventures.

smallbusiness.yahoo.com offers feature articles on a range of topics, small business news and stock quotes. Yahoo! Small Business also provides links to America's Business Funding Directory, *Entrepreneur* magazine, Quicken.com, and the SBA.

smalloffice.com has training, products, services, human resource material, and lots more. The site is well worth a visit and is related to *Home Office Computing*, a good magazine for small office/home office types.

smartonline.com provides useful information and sells small business services. Unlike its competitors, it doesn't surf for service providers, but offers its own software (the company started out as a small business software maker in 1993). Access to the site is free, as are downloadable business forms and some services including human resources, finance, and business-planning applications. More sophisticated applications cost $25 per use. The community section, with message boards, chat rooms, and opportunities to e-mail questions to experts, is useful.

toolkit.cch.com is Commerce Clearing House's site for small business owners. It provides a wide range of books, services, reviews, online workshops, forms, and other helpful material for small business owners. This is as close to a one-stop source as you will find.

uspto.gov belongs to the U.S. Patent and Trademark Office and offers information on patents and trademarks, along with necessary forms and fee schedules.

workingsolo.com is Terry Lonier's Web site. As the title implies, she is primarily interested in the solo practitioner, the one-person business. The site contains references and helpful links, as well as plugs for her book.

A Glossary of
Financial Terms

Accounting: The systematic recording, presenting, and interpreting of financial accounts.

Accounts payable: Amounts owed by a business to a creditor for goods and/or services.

Accounts receivable: Amounts owed to a business by its debtors for goods and/or services.

Accounts receivable turn: A ratio in which net credit sales are divided by average receivables. This provides a measure of the effectiveness of the company's collection procedures.

Accruals: An accounting method in which income and expenses are recorded as they are incurred, rather than when money changes hands. See *cash accounting.*

ACE-Net: The Small Business Administration's Angel Capital Electronic Network. You can find it at *www.sba.gov/advo/acenet.*

"Acid-test" ratio: {Cash + Receivables (net) + Marketable Securities} ÷ Current Liabilities. The "acid test" is one of the most important credit barometers used by lending institutions, as it indicates the ability of a business enterprise to meet its current obligations.

Aging receivables: A scheduling of accounts receivable according to the length of time they have been outstanding. This shows which accounts are not being paid in a timely manner and may reveal any difficulty in collecting long-overdue receivables. This may also be an important indicator of developing cash-flow problems.

Amortization: To liquidate on an installment basis; the process of gradually paying off a liability over a period of time; e.g., a mortgage is amortized by periodically paying off part of the face amount of the mortgage.

Angels: Private investors, usually with experience in the industry they invest in, who provide equity in amounts too small for professional investors (venture capitalists) to consider. See *ACE-Net.*

Assets: The valuable resources, or properties and property rights, owned by an individual or business enterprise.

Asset-turn ratio: Divide *sales* by *total assets.* This ratio measures whether your business is generating sufficient business given its asset base.

Balance sheet: An itemized statement that lists the total assets, liabilities, and net worth of a business to reflect its financial condition at a given moment in time.

Bookkeeping: The work of keeping a systematic record of financial transactions. The basis of the accounting system is recording these transactions in journals (daily entries), ledgers, and financial statements.

Bottom line: The bottom line on the income statement shows whether the company has made a profit, incurred a loss, or broken even after all expenses have been deducted from all revenues.

Break-even analysis: An analytic technique to determine exactly what sales level must be attained for the company to break even, that is, make neither a profit nor a loss. This involves the relation between fixed and variable costs. The break-even point is defined as: Fixed costs ÷ {1 − (variable expenses ÷ sales)}.

Budgeting: The most important financial activity for a small business. A budget attempts to establish a plan for adjusting expenses and disbursements during a certain period according to anticipated revenues.

Capital: Capital funds are those funds that are needed for the base of the business. Usually they are put into the business in a fairly permanent form such as in fixed assets, plant, and equipment, or are used in other ways that are not recoverable in the short run unless the entire business is sold.

Capital equipment: Equipment used to manufacture a product, provide a service, or to sell, store, and deliver merchandise. Such equipment will not be sold in the normal course of business but will be used and worn out or be consumed over time as business is conducted.

Capital gain: The difference between an asset's adjusted purchase price and selling price (assuming a gain). This has important tax implications that may affect your financing plans.

Capitalization structure: A corporation's financial structure, involving its long-term debt, preferred stock, and net worth.

Cash accounting: An accounting system in which sales and expenses are not recorded until cash changes hands.

Cash flow: The actual movement of cash within a business: cash inflow minus cash outflow. A term used to designate the reported net income of a corporation plus amounts charged off for depreciation, depletion, amortization, and extraordinary charges to reserves, which are bookkeeping deductions and not actually paid out in cash. Used to offer a better indication of the ability of a firm to meet its own obligations and to pay dividends, rather than the conventional net income figure.

Cash from receivables: Credit sales, where payment is postponed and you effectively grant credit to your customers, which will (we hope) eventually turn to cash. The decision to grant credit is a deeply involved and difficult one, and many business owners prefer not to issue credit themselves but rather dump the decision onto a bank by using one or more of the major credit cards. The banks, for a fee ranging from 1.5 to 7 percent or more, take on the credit and collection problems. Before you decide to issue credit, discuss the advisability of such a move with your banker and other financial advisors. You may find that competitive considerations force you to offer credit.

Cash position: See *liquidity*.

Collateral: An asset pledged to a lender in order to support a loan.

Collection period: Calculated by (receivables ÷ net sales) x 365 = collection period in days. This should be compared with your industry standard. If the standard is 30 days and your period is 25 days, great. If it is 45 days or more, your bankers will want to know why.

Comparative statements: A key element in analyzing financial statements involves comparisons with similar businesses, historical financial statements, and trade or industry averages such as the Robert Morris Associates' data. This makes it possible to compare performance across time and between different companies.

Compensating balance: Your banker may require that you use his or her bank as your company's primary bank of deposit as a condition of extending credit.

Contribution margin: Sales revenue – (cost of goods sold + all variable operating expenses).

Corporation: A legal entity that exists independently of the person or persons who created it. The decision to incorporate calls for professional advice from your lawyer and accountant, since there are many legal and tax ramifications.

Cost of capital: Rate of return that the business could earn if it chose another investment of equivalent risk. See *opportunity cost.*

Cost of goods sold (COGS): The cost of acquiring raw materials and producing finished goods.

Cumulative cash flow: For the first month, equals net cash flow. For subsequent months, equals previous month's cumulative cash flow plus new month's net cash flow. This is a particularly important figure, because it is used to calculate new capital and debt needs well in advance of the time those monies are needed in the business. If you can show a CCF to your banker and explain why you will need a loan five months hence, your chances of business success are greatly improved.

Current assets: Cash or other items that will normally be turned into cash within one year and assets that will be used up in the operations of a firm within one year.

Current liabilities: Amounts owed that will ordinarily be paid by a firm within one year. Such items include accounts payable, wages payable, taxes payable, the current portion of a long-term debt, and interest and dividends payable.

Current ratio: A ratio of a firm's current assets to its current liabilities. Because a current ratio includes the value of inventories that have not yet been sold, it does not offer the best evaluation of the firm's current status. The "acid-test" ratio, covering the most liquid of current assets, produces a better evaluation.

Debt: Debt refers to borrowed funds, whether from your own coffers or from other individuals, banks, or institutions. It is generally secured with a note, which in turn may be secured by a lien against property or other assets. Ordinarily, the note states repayment and interest provisions, which vary greatly in both amount and duration, depending upon the purpose, source, and terms of the loan. Some debt is convertible; that is, it may be changed into direct ownership of a portion of a business under certain stated conditions.

Debt-to-worth ratio: (Total debt ÷ total net worth), a ratio used to measure the amount of financial leverage a firm has. Used in comparison with similar firms in the same industry as a measure of the amount of risk involved in making a further investment.

Depreciation: A way to spread the cost of a capital good over its anticipated useful life; amortization of the cost of a fixed asset. Depreciation offsets income and reduces taxes. Check with your accountant to set up the appropriate depreciation schedules for your business.

Discounted cash flow: A dollar in hand now is worth more than a dollar you will get in the future (even ignoring the risks). The value of future expected cash receipts at a common date.

Dividend: Distribution of earnings to shareholders.

Double taxation: Corporations pay taxes on profits, and shareholders pay taxes on dividends.

EBIT: An acronym for "earnings before interest and taxes." This provides a measure of the capacity of a business to repay its obligations.

Employee stock ownership plan (ESOP): A program encouraging employees to purchase stock in the company they work for. There may be tax benefits; consult with your accountant.

Equipment: Usually limited to equipment used in the operation of the business. The IRS has become increasingly alert to the real uses of company-owned boats, planes, and other toys.

Equity: Equity is the owner's investment in the business. Unlike capital, equity is what remains after the liabilities of the company are subtracted from the assets; thus it may be greater than or less than the capital invested in the business. Equity investment carries with it a share of ownership and usually a share in profits, as well as some say in how the business is managed.

Extraordinary item: A nonrecurring item that must be explained to the owners, creditors, shareholders, or other interested parties in the financial statements for the period in which the item happens.

Factor: A factor purchases qualified accounts receivable, a form of financing that assists cash flow for companies with good though lengthy receivables.

Financial leverage: The balance between the owners' investment and debt indicates the degree of financial leverage. The higher the leverage, the higher the potential returns—but also the higher the risk. Financial leverage is an important investment criterion.

Financial statements: The major financial statements compiled from the general ledger are the income statement, the balance sheet, and the cash flow (or funds flow) statement. The cash-flow pro forma is often substituted for the funds flow in smaller companies.

Fixed assets: Assets that have an expected useful life of more than one year. Equipment, machinery, fixtures, and real estate are examples.

Fixed costs: Those costs that remain constant through a range of revenues. If revenues rise steeply, the fixed costs of plant and equipment (for example) tend to rise abruptly. Contrast with *variable costs.*

Free cash flow: Cash flow from profit available for whatever the management wishes.

General partner: One of two or more partners who are responsible (jointly and severally) for all debts of the partnership; managing partner of a limited partnership.

Goodwill: Excess of purchase price over book value (net worth minus subordinated debt) of the business. Applies only to a business that is purchased and demands your accountant's careful attention for tax reasons.

Gross income: Total personal income before deductions and exclusions.

Gross profit: Net sales (sales minus returned merchandise, discounts, or other allowances) minus the cost of goods sold, before deducting operating costs.

Guaranty: A pledge by a third party to repay a loan in the event the borrower cannot.

Hurdle rate: The required rate of return in a discounted cash flow analysis. If returns on a proposed investment won't equal or exceed the hurdle rate, the investment should not be made.

Income statement: A statement of income and expenses for a given period of time.

Internal rate of return (IRR): A trial-and-error process to determine whether the present value of future cash flows from a proposed investment equals the cost of the investment. This measure is used by venture capitalists and other sophisticated investors as part of their decision process.

Inventory: The materials owned and held by a business firm, including new materials, intermediate products and parts, work-in-process, and finished goods, intended either for internal consumption or for sale.

Inventory turn ratio: Sales ÷ inventory is a ratio to help you walk the tightrope between over- and understocking. Used by bankers to evaluate operating skills, especially in retail businesses.

Investment bank: A firm that acts as the intermediary between an issuer of securities and the investing public.

Leverage: Extent to which a company's costs of operating are fixed as opposed to variable. The degree of operating leverage measures the sensitivity of the firm's earnings to increases in revenue.

Liability: The debts of a business (payables, notes, debentures, etc.).

Limited Liability Corporation (LLC): A form of corporation offering the benefits of a corporation and the tax advantages of a partnership. As with any choice of business form, check with your lawyer and accountant.

Limited Liability Partnership (LLP): A partnership in which the limited partners' exposure is limited to the extent of their investment, while the managing partner has unlimited liability.

Limited partner: A partner in a limited partnership whose exposure is limited to the extent of his or her investment.

Line of credit: A commitment made by a bank to lend a company up to an agreed upon amount of money during a specified period, customarily one year, subject to review on any loan agreement in effect. A credit card is an example of an open-ended line of credit.

Liquid assets: Assets readily converted into cash such as notes and accounts receivable, money market funds, treasury bills, and so on. A measure of ability to meet short-term obligations.

Liquidity: A term used to describe the solvency of a business and that has special reference to the degree of readiness in which assets can be converted into cash without a loss. Also called *cash position*. If a firm's current assets cannot be converted into cash to meet current liabilities, the firm is said to be *illiquid*.

Loan agreement: A document that states what a business can or cannot do as long as it owes money to (usually) a bank. A loan agreement may place restrictions on the owner's salary or dividends, the amount of other debt, working capital limits, sales, or the number of additional personnel.

Loans: Debt money for private business is usually in the form of bank loans, which, in a sense, are personal because a private business can be harder to evaluate in terms of creditworthiness and degree of risk. A secured loan is a loan that is backed up by a claim against some asset or assets of a business. An unsecured loan is backed by the faith the bank has in the borrower's ability to pay back the money.

Loans from officers: Sometimes you have to put in more cash, but don't want to put it in permanently. There are also tax reasons (check with your accountant) that make this desirable.

Loans to officers (or draw): A major problem for small businesses is that the owners take out too much in salary, advances, and even loans from the company to themselves. A red flag to your banker and other creditors, and a sure way to have your business subjected to an IRS audit.

Long-term liabilities: These are liabilities (expenses) that will not mature within the next year.

Marketable securities: Banker's acceptances, government securities, and commercial paper. These are easily sold and converted to cash.

Merchant bank: A division of a bank that participated in investment banking activities.

Mezzanine financing: Financing provided just before a public offering. A relatively low-risk investment for venture capitalists.

"Near cash": Usually limited to liquid assets and marketable securities.

Net present value (NPV): The present value of a capital investment less the amount of capital invested. Positive NPV represents an investment opportunity, whereas a negative NPV suggests disinvestment.

Net worth: The owner's equity in a given business represented by the excess of the total assets over the total amounts owed to outside creditors (total liabilities) at a given moment in time. Also, the net worth of an individual as determined by deducting the amount of all his or her personal liabilities from the total value of his personal assets. Generally refers to tangible net worth (i.e., does not include goodwill, etc.).

Note: The basic business loan, a note represents a loan that will be repaid or substantially reduced 30, 60, or 90 days later at a stated interest rate. These are short term, and unless they are made under a line of credit, a separate loan application is needed for each loan and each renewal.

"Nut": Total monthly fixed expenses.

Operating expenses: Normal costs of doing business.

Operating profit or loss: Profit or loss from operations as opposed to investment or other profits or losses.

Opportunity cost of capital: The return on capital that could have been invested in another opportunity. Used in comparing ROA or ROI on alternative investments.

Partnership: A legal relationship created by the voluntary association of two or more persons to carry on as co-owners of a business for profit; a type of business organization in which two or more persons agree on the amount of their contributions (capital and effort) and on the distribution of profits, if any.

Present value: The value today of a future payment or stream of payments on a capital investment.

Prime rate: The interest rate on commercial loans charged by banks to their best and most creditworthy customers.

Principal: The unpaid balance of a loan or other obligation.

Profit: The excess of the selling price over all costs and expenses incurred in making a sale. Also, the reward to the entrepreneur for the risks assumed by him or her in the establishment, operations, and management of a given enterprise or undertaking.

Profit and loss statement (P&L): See *income statement.*

Pro forma: A projection or estimate of what may result in the future from actions in the present. A pro forma financial statement is one that shows how the actual operations of a business will turn out if certain assumptions are realized.

Quick ratio: (Cash + near cash) ÷ current liabilities. A measure of current liquidity. See *"acid-test" ratio.*

Retained earnings: One of your goals (in order to build tax-advantaged value in your business) is to retain the earnings in the business (in new assets, lower liabilities, and cash or cash equivalents). Ask your accountant about this if you find you have a lot of earnings to retain. There are tax implications. A negative retained earnings figure alarms your banker and other creditors, and is usually a sign that more capital is needed if the business is to survive and prosper.

Return on assets (ROA): (Net profit ÷ total assets), a measure of profitability indicating how well you are using your assets.

Return on equity (ROE): (Net profit ÷ owner's equity), a measure of profitability.

Return on investment (ROI): (Net profit ÷ net worth), a ratio used to measure profitability. It is erratic in thinly capitalized businesses.

Small Business Administration (SBA): The government's cabinet-level agency created in 1953 to provide loan guarantees and other small business services. The SBA 7(a) program guarantees up to 80 percent of a bank's loan to a qualifying small business.

Small Business Development Centers: The SBA established this program to provide technical assistance and other training to small business owners. The centers provide a very professional, discreet, and inexpensive service for small business owners.

Small Business Innovation Research (SBIR): A government program designed to stimulate potentially marketable research by smaller firms through research grants.

Small Business Investment Company (SBIC): Another SBA program, SBICs

finance the capital needs of growing businesses that are too small to be of interest to the major investment players (merchant banks, pension funds, venture capitalists, and so on). They may provide either debt or equity financing.

Sole proprietorship or *proprietorship:* A type of business organization in which one individual owns the business. Legally, the owner is the business and personal assets are typically exposed to liabilities of the business.

Special Small Business Investment Company (SSBIC): A variant of SBICs that provides financing to members of special groups: in particular; women, veterans, and minorities.

Spreadsheet analysis: Use of computerized spreadsheet programs such as Excel or Lotus makes careful financial analysis of financial statements much easier, removing the barriers to use of such complex calculations as IRR and NPV available to small business owners.

Sub-Chapter S corporation or *tax option corporation:* A corporation that has elected under Sub-Chapter S of the IRS Tax Code (by unanimous consent of its shareholders) not to pay any corporate tax on its income and, instead, to have the shareholders pay taxes on it, even though it is not distributed. Shareholders of a tax option corporation are also entitled to deduct, on their individual returns, their shares of any net operating loss sustained by the corporation, subject to limitations in the tax code. In many respects, Sub-Chapter S permits a corporation to behave for tax purposes as a proprietorship or partnership.

Subordinated debt: Your banker may ask you to subordinate your loan to bank debt. This means that in the event of a disaster the bank gets paid before you do. Also known as quasi-capital, because you can't pay yourself before the bank debt has been paid off (without permission of the bank). That means your loan to your business is locked in the way capital is.

Takeover: The acquisition of one company by another company.

Target market: The specific individuals, distinguished by socioeconomic, demographic, and/or interest characteristics, who are the most likely potential customers for the goods and/or services of a business.

Term loans: Either secured or unsecured, usually for periods of more than a year to as many as 10. Term loans are paid off like a mortgage: so many dollars per month for so many years. The most common uses of term loans are for equipment and other fixed asset purposes, for working capital, and for real estate.

Variable costs: Costs that fluctuate with the level of sales, rising or falling as sales rise or fall. Most obvious are costs such as sales commissions, delivery costs, and packaging.

Vehicles: Included in *equipment and machinery*. The "company car" is still popular, but if too costly becomes a red flag to the IRS.

Venture capital: The most sophisticated risk capital, concentrating on ventures promising very high potential returns (40 percent IRR) in a three-to-five-year horizon. The floor for venture capital is shifting toward larger amounts; the average is $7,000,000.

Weighted average cost of capital: See *hurdle rate.*

Working capital: The difference between current assets and current liabilities. Contrasted with capital, a permanent use of funds, working capital cycles through your business in a variety of forms: inventories, accounts and notes receivable, and cash and securities.

Index